DE PROPRIETATIBUS LITTERARUM

edenda curat

C. H. VAN SCHOONEVELD

Indiana University

Series Minor, 13

A GRAMMAR OF STORIES

An Introduction

by

GERALD PRINCE

University of Pennsylvania

1973

MOUTON

THE HAGUE · PARIS

Printed in Belgium by NICI, Ghent.

PREFACE

In this study I attempt to show that a finite number of explicit rules could account for the structure of all the sets and only the sets which are generally and intuitively recognized as stories. After an introduction studying the possibility of such a grammar and specifying its role, the first chapter describes the features common to all sets generally and intuitively recognized as stories through a definition of the minimal story. The second chapter develops a grammar capable of accounting for the structure of a specific kind of story, the kernel simple story. The third and fourth chapters show that the grammar of kernel simple stories, when complemented by other rules, could assign a structure to any set generally and intuitively recognized as a story. An appendix illustrates more concretely the possibilities of the grammar: the structure of Perrault's version of *Little Red Riding Hood* is described in terms of it. Finally, a short conclusion summarizes the results of the study.

In constructing a grammar of stories I have had to go over many well-known facts about stories and a few that are perhaps less well-known. Furthermore, I have followed very closely the early versions of the theory of generative grammar developed by Chomsky. For the sake of convenience, brevity, and clarity, I have often used as examples stories and non-stories of which I am the author. Such examples may not always be very satisfactory but this in no way invalidates the general lines along which the grammar is built.

I should like to thank Ellen F. Prince for many lengthy discussions of the material and many valuable suggestions. I should also like to thank Jean Alter, Carlos Lynes, Jr., and Russell P. Sebold.

This work was supported by a Faculty Research Grant from the University of Pennsylvania.

TABLE OF CONTENTS

Preface 5

Introduction 9

1. The Minimal Story 16

2. The Kernel Simple Story 38

3. The Simple Story 56

4. The Complex Story 71

Appendix 84

Conclusion 101

Bibliography 102

Index 105

INTRODUCTION

0.1 Everybody may not know how to tell good stories but every-body, in every human society known to history and anthropology, knows how to tell stories, and this at a very early age. Indeed, Barthes notes that "il peut être significatif que ce soit au même moment (vers l'âge de trois ans) que le petit de l'homme 'invente' à la fois la phrase, le récit et l'Oedipe".[1] Furthermore, everybody distinguishes stories from non-stories, that is, everybody has certain intuitions — or has internalized certain rules — about what constitutes a story and what does not. As Neumayer says, for instance, "human beings (even children) have tacit (unarticulated, they don't know they have it) knowledge that stories do resolve".[2] Finally, there is often agreement as to whether a given set of ele-ments constitutes a story or not:

(1) *A man was very happy, then he married a vain and domineering woman, then, as a result, he was very unhappy*

is a story, however trivial it may be. On the other hand,

(2) *Electrons are constituents of atoms,*

however interesting, is not. Indeed, people of widely different cultur-al backgrounds often identify the same given sets of elements as stories and reject others as non-stories, and they often tell stories

---

[1] Roland Barthes, "Introduction à l'analyse structurale des récits", *Communications*, no. 8 (1966), 27.
[2] Peter F. Neumayer, "The Child as Storyteller: Teaching Literary Concepts Through Tacit Knowledge", *College English*, XXX, no. 7 (1969), 517.

that are very similar. Thus, Russian and North American Indian folktales were shown to have many features in common.[3] It seems, therefore, that, to a certain extent at least, everybody has the same intuitions — or has internalized the same rules — about the nature of stories.

A grammar of stories is a series of statements or formulas describing these rules or, rather, capable of yielding the same results. A grammar should be explicit. It should indicate, with a minimum of interpretation left to its user, how a story can be produced by utilizing a specific set of rules and assign to such a story a structural description. It should also be complete and account for all and only possible stories, but this is probably an ideal to approximate rather than a reality at hand.[4] As for sets of elements which are recognized as stories by some and not by others, and there are undoubtedly many such sets, a grammar of stories could make clear what features these sets have in common with sets constituting fully acceptable stories and what features they do not have in common with them. It could also specify their degree of grammaticalness.[5]

0.1.1. In recent years, with the rediscovery of the Russian formalists and in particular of Propp, with the advent of structuralism and more specifically of structural anthropology, with the tremen-

---

[3] See Vladimir Propp, *Morphology of the Folktale* (Bloomington, 1958) and Alan Dundes, *The Morphology of North American Indian Folktales* (Helsinki, 1964).

[4] On requirements for grammars see, among others, Noam Chomsky, *Syntactic Structures* (The Hague, 1957) and, by the same author, "On the Notion 'Rule of Grammar'", *Proceedings of the Twelfth Symposium in Applied Mathematics*, XII (1961), 6-24; "Some Methodological Remarks on Generative Grammar", *Word*, XVII (1961), 219-223; "A Transformational Approach to Syntax", in A. A. Hill, ed., *Proceedings of the 1958 Conference on Problems of Linguistic Analysis in English* (Austin, Texas, 1962), 124-158; *Aspects of the Theory of Syntax* (Cambridge, Mass., 1965). See also Emmon Bach, *An Introduction to Transformational Grammars* (New York, 1964) and Paul Postal, *Constituent Structure. A Study of Contemporary Models of Syntactic Description* (The Hague, 1964).

[5] On the subject of degrees of grammaticalness, see Chomsky, "Some Methodological Remarks on Generative Grammar".

dous influence exercised by linguistics on disciplines such as folklore and literary criticism, several scholars have developed or have started to develop grammars of stories or of certain sets of stories.[6] Though the purpose of this study is not to examine critically these various efforts, all of which are highly interesting, it should be pointed out that the grammars built thus far are not explicit, or not complete, or both. Barthes and Tzvetan Todorov, for instance, fail to identify with precision the basic structural units of a story.

---

[6] See, for instance, Roland Barthes, "Introduction à l'analyse structurale des récits", 1-27; Claude Bremond's "Le Message narratif", *Communications*, no. 4 (1964), 4-32, "La logique des possibles narratifs", *Communications*, no. 8 (1966), 60-76, and "Postérité américaine de Propp", *Communications*, no. 11 (1968), 148-164; Eugene Dorfman's "The Structure of the Narrative: A Linguistic Approach", *History of Ideas Newsletter*, II (1956), 63-67 and *The Narreme in the Medieval Romance Epic: An Introduction to Narrative Structures* (Toronto, 1969); Alan Dundes' "Trends in Content Analysis: A Review Article", *Midwest Folklore*, XII, no. 1 (1962), 31-38, "From Etic to Emic Units in the Structural Study of Folktales", *Journal of American Folklore*, LXXV (1962), 95-105 and *The Morphology of North American Indian Folktales*; A. J. Greimas' *Sémantique structurale; recherche de méthode* (Paris, 1966), "Eléments pour une théorie de l'interprétation du récit mythique", *Communications*, no. 8 (1966), 28-59 and "La Structure des actants du récit. Essai d'approche générative", *Word*, XXIII, no. 1-2-3 (1967), 221-238; Elli K. Köngas and Pierre Maranda, "Structural Models in Folklore", *Midwest Folklore*, XII, no. 3 (1962), 133-192; Claude Lévi-Strauss, *Anthropologie structurale* (Paris, 1958); and Tzvetan Todorov's "Les Catégories du récit littéraire", *Communications*, no. 8 (1966), 125-151, *Littérature et signification* (Paris, 1967), "Poétique", in Oswald Ducrot et al., *Qu'est-ce que le structuralisme?* (Paris, 1968), 97-166, "La Grammaire du récit", *Langages*, no. 12 (1968), 94-102, *Grammaire du Décameron* (The Hague, 1970).
On the Russian Formalists, see Victor Erlich, *Russian Formalism: History-Doctrine* (The Hague, 1955) and Tzvetan Todorov, *Théorie de la littérature* (Paris, 1965). For an introduction to various attempts at building grammars of stories, see Michel Arrivé, "Stylistique littéraire et sémiotique littéraire", *La Nouvelle Critique*, no. spécial (1968), 171-174 and Jean Peytard, "Rapports et interférences de la linguistique et de la littérature (introduction à une bibliographie)", *La Nouvelle Critique*, no. spécial (1968), 8-16. For a description of various efforts to formalize the study of texts, see also Michel Arrivé, "Postulats pour la description linguistique des textes littéraires", *Langue Française*, no. 3 (1969), 3-13, William O. Hendricks, *Linguistics and the Structural Analysis of Literary Texts* (University of Illinois dissertation, 1965) and, by the same author, "On the Notion 'Beyond the Sentence'", *Linguistics*, no. 37 (1967), 12-51.

On the other hand, the model elaborated by Dundes can describe only a particular set of stories, the folktale.[7]

0.2   Stories may be expressed in a variety of ways. As a matter of fact, any given story may be rendered through language, film, pantomime, and so on. Bremond puts it very well:

Le sujet d'un conte peut servir d'argument pour un ballet, celui d'un roman peut être porté à la scène ou à l'écran, on peut raconter un film à ceux qui ne l'ont pas vu. Ce sont des mots qu'on lit, ce sont des images qu'on voit, ce sont des gestes qu'on déchiffre, mais à travers eux, c'est une histoire qu'on suit; et ce peut être la même histoire. Le *raconté* a ses signifiants propres, ses *racontants:* ceux-ci ne sont pas des mots, des images ou des gestes, mais les événements, les situations et les conduites signifiés par ces mots, ces images, ces gestes.[8]

Suppose a given story is expressed in written language. This language may be English:

(3)   *John was very happy, then war came, then, as a result, John was very unhappy.*

It may also be French:

(4)   *Jean était très heureux puis la guerre éclata et Jean devint très malheureux,*

or any other written language.

Suppose a given story is in English. It may look like

(5)   *The people were happy, then war came, then, as a result, they were unhappy,*

---

[7]   Several of the grammars mentioned have been criticized in more or less detail. Thus, Dundes has criticized Lévi-Strauss in *The Morphology of North American Indian Folktales*, 42-47; Bremond has shown some of the weaknesses of Propp's and Dundes' morphologies of the folktale in "Le Message narratif" and "Postérité américaine de Propp"; and Denis Guenoun has examined the works of Barthes, Bremond, and Todorov in "A propos de l'analyse structurale des récits", *La Nouvelle Critique*, no. spécial (1968), 65-70.

[8]   Claude Bremond, "Le message narratif", 4. On this subject, see also Barthes, "Introduction à l'analyse structurale des récits", 1 and Dundes, "Trends in Content Analysis: A Review Article", 36 and *The Morphology of North American Indian Folktales*, 44.

or

(6) *The people were happy, then war came, then, as a result,*
     the people were unhappy,

or still another paraphrase of (5).

Finally, note that non-stories, for instance the description of an English castle, may likewise be rendered through language or film, English or French, and so forth.

Consequently, it can be said that neither the substance (sounds, images, gestures, etc.) nor the form (certain specific English sentences, for instance) of the expression side of a story defines it as a story rather than a non-story. This is why a grammar of stories does not have to be concerned with the description of the expression side of stories.[9]

0.3 A story may deal with any number of subjects and any number of themes. There are stories about love, death, money, trees, birds, and so on. There are even stories about stories. Moreover, a story, a poem, or an essay may have the same subject and deal with the same themes. There are stories about Napoleon; there are also poems and essays about him. It is clear therefore that the subject of a story and the themes it deals with do not define it as a story rather than a non-story, which is why a grammar of stories does not have to be concerned with the study of subjects and themes.

0.4   Let us assume that we have a certain number of content units, each one represented by a certain string of symbols. Suppose, for instance, that:

content unit A = *John was happy*

[9] For the sake of convenience, the stories I use as examples are all verbal and the rules I propose are derived from these verbal stories. This does not mean that the rules proposed cannot be applied to non-verbal stories or that the concepts they express are not transferable to such stories. Even a concept such as causality can be applied to a story expressed through a series of dances; and, if a ballet does not imply causality, its storyness – should it have any – is decreased.

content unit B = *John met a woman*
content unit C = *John was unhappy*
content unit D = *John went to the movies*
content unit E = *John ate an apple*
content unit F = *John ate a pear*
content unit G = *then*
content unit H = *and*
content unit I   = *as a result.*

A group of five units arranged according to pattern P constitutes what we would intuitively recognize as a story:

(7) *John was happy, then John met a woman, then, as a result, John was unhappy.*

A group of the same units arranged according to another pattern P' constitutes a different story:

(8) *John was unhappy, then John met a woman, then, as a result, John was happy.*

On the other hand, a group of the same units arranged according to still another pattern P'' does not constitute a story:

(9) *John was happy, then, as a result, John was unhappy, then John met a woman.*

Nor does a different group of five units arranged according to any random pattern. Consider, for instance:

(10) *John ate an apple and John ate a pear and then John went to the movies*

(11) *John ate a pear and John ate an apple and then John went to the movies*

(12) *John went to the movies and then John ate an apple and John ate a pear.*

We can summarize the preceding by saying that a group of content units selected at random and arranged in a random fashion does not necessarily constitute a story. Only groups of content units having certain features and arranged according to certain patterns constitute what would intuitively and generally be recognized as a story. A grammar of stories should describe and account for all such groups and only such groups.

0.5   Such a grammar, if properly refined, would not only characterize explicitly and formally the most essential features of stories and provide a powerful tool for the description of the structure of a given story, it would also constitute a valuable heuristic device and lead to a better understanding of the nature of stories. Furthermore, it would allow for a precise typology of stories according to their structure. It would, moreover, help solve many questions concerning stories: is the structure of folktales significantly different from that of more 'sophisticated' stories? what kinds of stories — in terms of structure — does a given society favor? why? Finally, it may have interesting implications for studies of thinking and learning processes or studies of emotional disturbances: why are some story structures which are theoretically possible according to the grammar rarely — if ever — encountered in practice? what stages does a child go through in developing his ability to tell stories? does an emotionally disturbed child consistently favor certain structural patterns that a normal child would not favor? A grammar of stories may thus ultimately deepen not only our understanding of the nature of stories but also our understanding of man.

1. THE MINIMAL STORY

1.0 A rigorous analysis of any structure presupposes the identification of the discrete units making up that structure, for only when these units have been isolated properly is it possible to describe the way they are distributed and combined in order to yield that structure. If we consider a story to be made up of a certain number of units combined in a certain way, we first have to give an explicit definition of these units meeting certain formal standards and allowing us to determine them as easily and unambiguously as possible.

One of the weaknesses of the interesting and useful work done by such scholars as Propp, Barthes, or Tzvetan Todorov is the lack of explicit criteria for the identification of the basic units that constitute a story. Propp does not specify the exact relation between his structural unit, the function, and its (linguistic) representation. Barthes gives what is at best a sketchy definition of the basic elements of a story:

[il y a] deux grandes classes de fonctions, les unes distributionnelles, les autres intégratives. Les premières correspondent aux fonctions de Propp, reprises notamment par Bremond, mais que nous considérons ici de façon infiniment plus détaillée que ces auteurs; c'est à elles que l'on réservera le nom de *'fonctions'* (bien que les autres unités soient, elles aussi, fonctionnelles); le modèle en est classique depuis l'analyse de Tomachevski: l'achat d'un revolver a pour corrélat le moment où l'on s'en servira (et si l'on ne s'en sert pas, la notation est retournée en signe de velléitarisme, etc.)... La seconde grande classe d'unités, de nature intégrative, comprend tous les *'indices'*... l'unité renvoie alors, non à un acte complémentaire et conséquent, mais à un concept plus

ou moins diffus, nécessaire cependant au sens de l'histoire: indices
caractériels concernant les personnages, information relatives à leur
identité, notations d'atmosphères, etc...[1]

Furthermore, he admits that it is often impossible to describe a
story strictly in terms of these units: "il semble pourtant que, si
l'analyse se veut exhaustive ... elle doive fatalement rencontrer
des notations qu'aucune fonction (même la plus indirecte qui
soit) ne permet de justifier ...".[2] As for Tzvetan Todorov, in order
to establish a grammar of the *Decameron*, he begins by summa-
rizing Boccacio's tales to reach what he feels are the main elements
of their plots. However, he does not explain specifically how one
should summarize a given tale.[3]

If we assume that the basic units constituting any story are
units of content, which I will call *events* for lack of a better term,
how are we to define an event? As mentioned in 0.2, any story
may be expressed through language. More specifically, it may be
represented by a series of (conjoined) sentences, each sentence
being the transform of at least one, but less than two, discrete
elementary string. From now on, I shall call *event* in a story any
part of that story which can be expressed by a sentence, where
sentence is taken to be the transform of at least one, but less than
two, discrete elementary string.[4] According to this definition, in
a given story,

(1)   *A man laughs*

would represent one event since it is the transform of a single
elementary string,

[1]   Roland Barthes, "Introduction à l'analyse structurale des récits", 8-9.
[2]   Roland Barthes, "L'Effet de réel", *Communications*, no. 11 (1968), 84.
[3]   See Tzvetan Todorov, "Poétique", 132-138.
[4]   For a similar proposal, see Charles T. Scott, "On Defining the Riddle: The
Problem of a Structural Unit", *Genre*, II, no. 2 (1969), 137. See also Gerald
Prince, "Towards a Normative Criticism of the Novel", *Genre*, II, no. 1
(1968), 8. For a discussion of transforms of elementary strings, see Chomsky's
Syntactic Structures and "A Transformational Approach to Syntax".
   Note that in the course of this study, and for the sake of convenience, I may
represent an event by a sentence which is not the transform of a single ele-
mentary string.

(2) *The man said that the boy laughed*

would also represent one event since it is not derived from two discrete elementary strings. On the other hand,

(3) *The boy who is here is nice*

would represent two events since it is derived from the transforms of two discrete elementary strings:

(4) *A boy is nice*

and

(5) *The boy is here.*

As for

(6) *a boy*

it would express no event since it is not a sentence.

Just as an event can be expressed by a sentence, a series of conjoined events constituting a story can be expressed by a series of conjoined sentences. In a given story, the following:

(7) *A man laughed and a woman cried*

would represent two conjoined events; and

(8) *A man laughed, then, as a result, a woman cried and a bird sang*

would represent three conjoined events.

Events are conjoined by conjunctive features. A conjunctive feature in a story is any part of that story which can be represented by a conjunctive term, where conjunctive term is taken to be any part of language serving to connect sentences. In (7), *and* is a conjunctive term and represents a conjunctive feature, and in (8), *then, as a result,* and *and* are conjunctive terms representing conjunctive features.

1.1 Every story contains at least one minimal story. I shall call *minimal story* any story which contains no member of the set of all stories as a proper part of it. In other words, a minimal story is equivalent to the smallest series of events conjoined by the minimum number of conjunctive features and constituting a story.

It is obvious that

(9) *An ax is a tool*

is not a story. Nor are:

(10) *A man is here*

(11) *A woman laughs*

Indeed, no sentence expressing one event and only one can ever represent a story. One may say, therefore, that no story is constituted by a single event and that a minimal story consists of more than one event.

On the other hand,

(12) *A man was happy, then he met a woman, then, as a result, he was very unhappy*

and

(13) *A man was very sick, then he ate an apple, then, as a result, he was forever very healthy*

would intuitively be recognized as stories, although not particularly good ones. Since (12) and (13) are made up of three conjoined sentences, each sentence representing one event, we may say that no more than three conjoined events are required to constitute a story.

Could a story be constituted by two conjoined events? Consider the following set of discourses made up of two conjoined sentences, each sentence representing one event and only one:

(14) *John tortured Mary and Mary tortured Jack*
(15) *John was handsome and Paul ate bananas*
(16) *John was rich and he was miserable*
(17) *John was rich then he was poor*
(18) *John tortured Mary then he tortured Jack*
(19) *John murdered Paul because Paul was hateful*
(20) *John was European but Peter was African*

(21) *John was happy although Mary was poor*

(22) *John was French therefore he was European.*

Clearly, none of these discourses constitutes a story. Nor would any discourse made up of two conjoined sentences, each sentence expressing one event and only one. Consequently, it may be said that two conjoined events cannot constitute a story.

The smallest number of conjoined events required to constitute a story is three and the minimal story is a story consisting of three conjoined events. It should be noted that several scholars, using different approaches, have arrived at similar conclusions. For example, Bremond writes: "Un premier groupement de trois fonctions engendre la *séquence élémentaire*. Cette triade correspond aux trois phases obligées de tout processus ...".[5]

1.2.0 In order to conjoin three events, no more than two conjunctive features are needed:

(23) *The sun was shining and the birds were singing, then it rained*

(24) *John ate an apple, then he went to bed because he was tired.*

Furthermore, the two conjunctive features may be identical, i.e., representable by two identical or synonymous conjunctive terms:

(25) *John loved Mary and Mary loved Jim and Jim loved Joan*

(26) *Socrates was good and he was intelligent and he was courageous*

(27) *Condé won a battle, then Turenne won one, then Luxembourg lost one*

(28) *The sun rose, then it shone, then it set.*

On the other hand, more than one conjunctive feature may conjoin two events, and more than two may conjoin three events:

(29) *John was happy but then he became sad*

---

[5] Bremond, "La Logique des possibles narratifs", 60. On this subject, see also Bremond, "Postérité américaine de Propp", 152; A. J. Greimas, *Sémantique structurale*, 202-203; and Violette Morin, "L'Histoire drôle", *Communications*, no. 8 (1966), 102.

(30) *John was happy but then he became sad, then, as a result,
Peter was happy.*

We have determined that no more than three conjoined events
are required to constitute a minimal story. We now have to determine how many conjunctive features are needed to conjoin these
three events and whether two or more of them may be identical.
Consider the following (trivial!) stories, made up of three conjoined
events:

(31) *A man was unhappy, then he fell in love, then, as a result,
he was happy*

(32) *A woman was ugly, then a magician helped her, then, as a
result, she was beautiful*

(33) *John was very chaste, then he met Mary, then, as a result,
he was promiscuous.*

In each of the three stories, the first event is conjoined with the
second by one conjunctive feature (the minimum number capable
of conjoining two events) and the second is conjoined with the
third by two conjunctive features, one of which is identical to the
first conjunctive feature. All in all, there are three conjunctive
features, two of which are identical, in each of the stories.

Is it possible to have a smaller number of conjunctive features
in a minimal story? Consider the following set of discourses
representing three events conjoined by two conjunctive features:

(34) *A man was unhappy, therefore he was happy, then he fell in love*

(35) *John was chaste, therefore he was promiscuous, then he met
Mary*

(36) *A man was unhappy, then he fell in love, then he was happy*

(37) *John was chaste, then he met Mary, then he was promiscuous.*

(34) and (35) are obviously not stories. As for (36) and (37), rather
than stories, they are mere enumerations of a series of events.
Similarly, any three events conjoined by only two conjunctive

features would not constitute a story. I will therefore tentatively define a minimal story as consisting of three events conjoined in such a way that the first is joined to the second by one conjunctive feature and the second is joined to the third by two conjunctive features, one of which is identical to the first conjunctive feature.

1.2.1 Not any three events thus conjoined constitute a minimal story. Consider the following examples:

(38) *John was rich, then he travelled a lot, then, as a result, he was poor*

(39) *John was very sad, then he saw Mary, then, as a result, he was very happy*

(40) *John was rich and he travelled a lot, then, as a result, he was poor*

(41) *John was rich and he travelled a lot but then he became poor*

(42) *John danced and Bill sang and yet Jim smoked.*

(38) and (39) constitute stories whereas (40), (41), and (42) do not. The first two examples differ from the others in at least one way. In both of them, the conjunctive features indicate that each event happens at a different time. More particularly, they indicate that the three events are in chronological order, the first event occurring before the second in time, and the second before the third. In the other examples, the conjunctive features establish no such relationship between the events: two out of the three events in (40) and (41) and all three in (42) are cotemporaneous.[6]

We may therefore further define the minimal story as consisting of three events conjoined in such a way that (a) the first is joined to the second by one conjunctive feature and the second is joined to the third by two conjunctive features, one of which is identical

---

[6] For a further discussion of temporal sequence in stories, see 2.2.1-2.2.1.1, 3.1-3.1.3.1, and 3.6.

to the first conjunctive feature, and (b) the first event precedes
the second in time and the second precedes the third.[7]

1.2.1.1 Probably every student of stories has underlined the
importance of the role played by chronology in them. As Greimas
puts it:

L'unité discursive qu'est le récit est à considérer comme un *algorithme*,
c'est-à-dire, comme une succession d'énoncés dont les fonctions-pré-
dicats simulent linguistiquement un ensemble de comportements ayant
un but. En tant que succession, le récit possède une dimension tempo-
relle: les comportements qui s'y trouvent étalés entretiennent entre eux
des relations d'antériorité et de postériorité.[8]

Indeed, ordering of events in time is one of the most fundamental
characteristics of any story. Given a (non-minimal) story with a
certain number of characteristics, one may eliminate from it
many of these characteristics and still obtain a story. But one can
never eliminate from it the characteristic 'ordering of events in
time' without completely destroying it as a story: "Tout récit
consiste en un discours intégrant une succession d'événements
d'intérêt humain dans l'unité d'une même action. Où il n'y a
pas succession, il n'y a pas récit...".[9] A good case in point is
provided by those practitioners of the New Novel who want, among
other things, to write storyless novels and who achieve this goal
by making it impossible for the reader to establish any chronology
of events. In Robbe-Grillet's *La Jalousie*, for instance, the crushing
of the centipede which, in a novel telling a story, would provide a
good point of reference around which to situate the other events
in time, is made to occur before the trip taken by Frank and A.,
during their trip, and after it.

[7] Or, more precisely, in such a way that the beginning of the first event
precedes in time the beginning of the second event and that the end of the second
event precedes in time the end of the third.
[8] A. J. Greimas, "Eléments pour une théorie de l'interprétation du récit
mythique", 29. Many scholars have studied in detail the role of time in stories.
See, for instance, Robert Champigny, *Le Genre romanesque* (Monte-Carlo,
1963), A. A. Mendilow, *Time and the Novel* (London, 1952), and Jean Pouillon,
Temps et roman (Paris, 1946).
[9] Bremond, "La Logique des possibles narratifs", 62.

1.2.2 Not any three events conjoined in such a way that (a) the first is joined to the second by one conjunctive feature and the second is joined to the third by two conjunctive features, one of which is identical to the first conjunctive feature, and (b) the first event precedes the second in time and the second precedes the third, constitute a minimal story. Consider the following examples:

(43) *John was rich, then he lost a lot of money, then, however, he was poor*

(44) *John was poor, then he earned a lot of money, then, however, he was rich*

(45) *John was rich, then he lost a lot of money, then, as a result, he was poor*

(46) *John was poor, then he earned a lot of money, then, as a result he was rich.*

(43) and (44) would not be recognized as stories whereas (45) and (46) would. The difference between (43)-(44) on the one hand and (45)-(46) on the other is that, in the latter, the third conjunctive feature indicates that the second and third events are related not only chronologically but also causally.

The definition of a minimal story must be further modified to indicate this causal relationship. A minimal story consists of three events conjoined in such a way that (a) the first event precedes the second in time and the second precedes the third, and (b) the second event causes the third. No more than three conjunctive features, one conjoining the first event with the second and two conjoining the second event with the third, are necessary.

1.2.2.1 The causal relationship between certain events is just as essential a feature of stories as the chronological one. In the twentieth century, novelists who want to write storyless or quasi-storyless novels whether because, like Sartre, they wish to present an absurd world in which there are no connections between events, or because, like Robbe-Grillet and Beckett, they try to create so-called pure novels, novels that are nothing but novels, systematically exclude from their fiction most logical bonds between events or groups of events. In *La Nausée*, for instance, Roquentin's visit to the museum is not caused by the events preceding it and does not cause the events following it. Rather than a logical arrangement, Sartre adopts a strictly temporal one. Roquentin thinks about Anny, then he goes to the Bouville museum, then he decides to stop writing his biography of M. de Rollebon.[10]

Perhaps it is Camus' *L'Etranger* which, better than any other novel, underlines the importance causality can have in a story. *L'Etranger* is divided in two parts, one recounting a series of events in Meursault's life and the other telling a very coherent story about him. In the first part, the protagonist goes through a series of experiences connected mainly because they follow one another in time and because he is at the centre of each of them. Meursault attends his mother's funeral, he sees a Fernandel movie, he makes love to Marie, he goes to the beach, he kills an Arab. His life is absurd, made up mostly of disparate events, and his murder of the Arab is without reason. In the second part, his judges, in order to inculpate him, try to fit his various experiences into a tightly-knit story the culmination of which is the murder of the Arab. They do it by multiplying causal relationships among them.[11]

1.2.2.2 One interesting feature of the causal relationship between two events occurring in a minimal story is that it must be accompanied by a chronological one, whereas the reverse is not true. For instance, in minimal stories (45) and (46) above, we have:

(47) *He lost a lot of money, then, as a result, he was poor*

(48) *He earned a lot of money, then, as a result, he was rich,*

but

(49) *John was rich, then he lost a lot of money*

[10] On the absence of causality in Sartre's fiction, see Gerald Prince, *Métaphysique et technique dans l'œuvre romanesque de Sartre* (Genève, 1968), 46-47.
[11] *L'Etranger* is not the only novel by Camus to deal with the nature of stories. After all, *La Chute* is, among many other things, the story of the tribulations of a storyteller.

(50) *John was poor, then he earned a lot of money.*

Any story must have at least two events which not only occur at different times but also are causally related. Usually, stories include many more events meeting this requirement. As a matter of fact, one of the main characteristics of (most) stories is that temporal sequence and logical consequence are often equated. As Barthes says: "Tout laisse à penser, en effet, que le ressort de l'activité narrative est la confusion même de la consécution et de la conséquence, ce qui vient *après* étant lu dans le récit comme *causé par*; le récit serait, dans ce cas, une application systématique de l'erreur logique dénoncée par la scolastique sous la formule *post hoc, ergo propter hoc...*".[12] The equation is not difficult to accomplish. It is not pure coincidence that, in English, *then* can be used to imply both chronology:

(51) *He got up then sat down*

and consequence:

(52) *If he is rich, then he is no good*

and that *alors* can do the same in French.

1.2.2   Given any discourse representing a minimal story, it can be defined in part as indicating a specific organization of the events represented by its sentences: chronological order of the first and second events, chronological and logical order of the second and third. Similarly, any other kind of discourse can be at least partially defined by the order of events it indicates, whether it be a chronological order, or a logical one, or what may be called a spatial one (if the conjunctive term used is *and* rather than *then* or *as a result*), etc. Thus, annals and chronicles indicate that some events are ordered chronologically and others spatially, and pure poetic discourse reveals a mere spatial order of events.[13]

[12]   Barthes, "Introduction à l'analyse structurale des récits", 10. See also Tzvetan Todorov, "Poétique", 123ff.
[13]   The most fundamental difference between poetic discourse and any other kind of discourse is that in the former the sentences *are* the events. Poetic discourse is what it represents and represents what it is.

1.2.3 Not any three events conjoined in such a way that (a) the first event precedes the second in time and the second precedes the third, and (b) the second event causes the third, constitute a minimal story. Consider the following examples:

(53) *John was rich, then he ate an apple, then, as a result, he went to Germany*

(54) *John was rich, then he lost a lot of money, then, as a result, he met a woman*

(55) *John was happy, then he met a woman, then, as a result, he went to Germany*

(56) *John was happy, then he met a woman, then, as a result, he ate an apple*

(57) *John was rich, then he lost a lot of money, then, as a result, he was poor*

(58) *John was happy, then he ate an apple, then, as a result, he was unhappy.*

(53)-(56) do not constitute stories but rather relate in a chronological and (partially) logical order a series of events having one actor in common. (57) and (58) also relate a series of events having one actor in common; however, they are intuitively recognized as stories.

According to many scholars, one of the characteristics of any story is that it must be a whole, an autonomous structure conveying, in some way, the impression that it is closed. Thus, Tzvetan Todorov, trying to define a story as a certain type of syntagmatic arrangement of events, writes: "Le second [type de segment] sera appelé *séquence*: il est formé de plusieurs propositions ... et donne au lecteur l'impression d'un tout achevé, d'une histoire, d'une anecdote".[14] (57) and (58) convey that impression whereas

---

For interesting discussions of various kinds of discourses see, among others, Kenneth L. Pike's "Discourse Analysis and Tagmeme Matrices", *Oceanic Linguistics*, III, no. 1 (1964) and *Language in Relation to a Unified Theory of the Structure of Human Behavior* (The Hague, 1967).

[14] Tzvetan Todorov, "Poétique", 133.

(53)-(56) do not. Clearly, it is not very difficult to determine with precision at least one of the reasons for the difference between (53)-(56) and (57)-(58). In the latter group, it is obvious that the third event is the inverse of the first, while in the former it is not.[15]

We can now define a minimal story as consisting of three events, the third of which is the inverse of the first. The three events are conjoined in such a way that (a) the first event precedes the second in time and the second precedes the third, and (b) the second event causes the third.

1.2.3.1 Several detailed studies of specific corpora of stories show that the inversion of an event is one of the essential features of a story. Both Propp and Dundes demonstrate for instance that, if in a given folktale there is a situation denoting a lack of some sort, this situation will be replaced by another one indicating that the lack has been liquidated.[16] Similarly, Tzvetan Todorov, describing the structure of three of Boccacio's tales, arrives at a formulation which shows very clearly that one element is the inverse of another:

$$
Y \begin{cases} \text{nuit à X} \\ \\ \text{a un défaut interne} \end{cases} + \text{X attaque Y} \rightarrow Y \begin{cases} \text{ne nuit plus à X} \\ \\ \text{n'a plus ce défaut.}^{17} \end{cases}
$$

1.2.3.2 Maybe the most fundamental difference between a historical discourse and a discourse representing a story is that the former does not require any event in it to be the inverse of another one. It can be, for instance, a mere recording of events in their

---

[15] Note that *inverse* is of course not equivalent to *negative*. Thus, in
(59) *On Tuesday, he played baseball; on Wednesday, he did not*
the second event is not the inverse of the first, whereas in
(60) *He was happy, then he was unhappy*
the second event is.
[16] See Propp's *Morphology of the Folktale* and Dundes' *The Morphology of North American Indian Folktales*.
[17] Tzvetan Todorov, "Poétique", 133-135.

chronological order. Of course, there often is in history an event which is the inverse of another one, and the historian who wants to make history meaningful or exciting often underlines such inversions: he tells the story of Napoleon, the story of the Franco-Prussian War, the story of the Third Reich. Similarly, a storyteller often chooses not to stress the fact that one event in his story is the inverse of another one in order to give the impression that his story is not fiction but history.

1.2.4   Not any three events, the third of which is the inverse of the first, and conjoined in such a way that (a) the first event precedes the second in time and the second precedes the third, and (b) the second event causes the third, constitute a story. Consider the following:

(61) *He opened the door, then he saw Mary, then, as a result, he closed the door*

(62) *He moved forward, then he was happy, then, as a result, he moved backward*

(63) *He was happy, then he was red, then, as a result, he was unhappy*

(64) *He was unhappy, then he met a woman, then, as a result, he was happy*

(65) *He was rich, then he lost a lot of money, then, as a result, he was poor.*

Of the above, (64) and (65) are the only examples which would intuitively be recognized as stories. They are also the only ones in which the first and third events describe states and the second describes an action.

1.2.4.1   From now on, I shall call *stative* event any event which describes a state and *active* event any event which describes an action. In 1.0, I defined an event in a story as any part of that story which can be expressed by a sentence. I will now define a stative event in a story as any part of that story which can be expressed

by a stative sentence, the latter being one which is not paraphrasable
by a sentence of the form *NP's V-ing NP Aux be an act*.[18]
    According to my definition,

(66) *John was happy*

and

(67) *John had a lot of money*

are both stative sentences since (66) is not paraphrasable by

(68) *John's being happy was an act*

and (67) is not paraphrasable by

(69) *John's having a lot of money was an act.*

In a given story, (66) and (67) would each represent a stative event.
On the other hand,

(70) *John ate an apple*

and

(71) *John listened to the music*

are both active sentences since (70) is paraphrasable by

(72) *John's eating an apple was an act*

and (71) is paraphrasable by

(73) *John's listening to the music was an act.*

In a given story, (70) and (71) would each represent an active event.

1.2.4.2   Consider the following:

(74) *John harmed Peter's brother; then Peter was very angry;
     then, as a result, Peter harmed John's brother.*

(74) would certainly be recognized as a story and it has many

---

[18]   On this subject, see Ellen F. Prince, "*Be-ing*: A Synchronic and Diachronic
Study", *Transformations and Discourse Analysis Papers*, no. 81 (University of
Pennsylvania, 1970).

features in common with (64) and (65): its events are conjoined
in such a way that (a) the first precedes the second in time and the
second precedes the third, and (b) the second event causes the third;
furthermore, the third event is the inverse of the first. Yet, unlike
what we find in (64) and (65), the first and third events are active
and the second event stative. Does this mean that a minimal
story could either consist of three events, the first and third of
which are stative and the second active, or of three events, the
first and third of which are active and the second stative? The
answer is negative, for (74) is not a minimal story. It is a story in
which three events are expressed, but it is not a three-event story
because it can be shown that some of its events have been zeroed.
(74) is simply a transform of

(75) *John harmed Peter's brother, then, as a result, Peter's brother*
     was John's victim; then Peter was very angry; then, as a result,
     Peter harmed John's brother, then, as a result, John's brother
     was Peter's victim

which is not a minimal story.[19]

Note that any story of the same type as (74) can be shown to be
a non-nimimal story, whereas this is not the case with any story
of the same type as (64) or (65). Note also that the presence of
two stative events in minimal stories confirms an intuition about
stories which Todorov expressed as follows: "L'intrigue minimale
complète consiste dans le passage d'un équilibre à un autre".[20]

1.2.5 A minimal story consists of three conjoined events. The
first and third events are stative, the second is active. Furthermore,
the third event is the inverse of the first. Finally, the three events
are conjoined by three conjunctive features in such a way that (a)
the first event precedes the second in time and the second precedes
the third, and (b) the second event causes the third.

---

[19] For a discussion of zeroing and the zeroing transformation, see 3.3-3.3.2
and 3.6.
[20] Tzvetan Todorov, "La Grammaire du récit", 96.

1.3   Just as a grammar of English can be built to account for the structure of all English sentences and only English sentences, a grammar can be built to account for the structure of all minimal stories and only minimal stories.[21] This grammar will consist of a set of symbols interrelated by an ordered set of rules, each rule being of the form X → Y (to be read: Rewrite X as Y) and only one rule being applied at a time. The rules obey the following restrictions: a) only one symbol can be rewritten in any single rule; b) the symbol to be rewritten and the replacing string may not be null; c) the symbol to be rewritten and the replacing string may not be identical; d) no rules of the form A → A + B (or A → B + A) may be used.

For the sake of brevity and an easier handling of the rules, I will use the following set of symbols:

M St	=	Minimal Story
E	=	event
E stat	=	stative event
E act	=	active event
In E stat	=	initial stative event
In E stat^{-1}	=	inverse of initial stative event
S stat	=	stative sentence
S stat^{-1}	=	inverse of stative sentence
S act	=	active sentence
CCL	=	cluster of conjunctive features, indicating that two events are conjoined by one or more conjunctive features
CF	=	conjunctive feature
CF$_t$	=	conjunctive feature indicating that two events are conjoined in such a way that the first precedes the second in time

---

[21]   In constructing my grammar, I follow Chomsky's *Syntactic Structures*, "On the Notion 'Rule of Grammar'", 6-24, and "A Transformational Approach to Syntax", 124-158; Emmon Bach, *An Introduction to Transformational Grammars*; Paul Postal, *Constituent Structure: A Study of Contemporary Models of Syntactic Description*, except when the restrictions imposed on phrase-structure rules do not apply.

CF_c = conjunctive feature indicating that two events are conjoined in such a way that the first causes the second

CT_t = conjunctive term indicating chronology

CT_c = conjunctive term indicating cause.

The sign $+$ indicates the concatenation of the various symbols in a string and may be suppressed where there is no danger of confusion.

Parentheses are used to enclose optionally chosen items. For the two rules

$A \rightarrow B$
$A \rightarrow B + C$
(but not $A \rightarrow C$)

we may write

$A \rightarrow B \ (C)$

Alternative replacements for a symbol, one of which may be chosen at a single application, are listed vertically within braces. Thus, for the three rules

$A \rightarrow B$
$A \rightarrow C$
$A \rightarrow D$

we may write

$$A \rightarrow \begin{Bmatrix} B \\ C \\ D \end{Bmatrix}$$

If we wish to allow a replacement for a given nonterminal symbol (a symbol appearing on the left of the arrow) in certain contexts only, we specify it in the appropriate rule. For instance, if A may be rewritten as B only when it is in initial position in any given string of symbols, we have the following rule:

$A \rightarrow B \ / \ ^\# \ \_\_$

If A may be rewritten as B only when it is in final position in any given string of symbols, we have the rule:

$$A \rightarrow B / \_\_ ^{\#}$$

If A may be rewritten as B only when it does not precede or immediately follow C, we have the rule:

$$A \rightarrow B / C + ... + \_\_$$

In all cases, $\_\_$ shows the place where the given replacement is allowed.

1.4   The rules constituting the grammar of minimal stories are the following:

1. $\text{M St} \rightarrow E + CCL + E + CCL + E$

2. $E \rightarrow \begin{cases} \text{E stat} / ^{\#} \_\_ \\ \text{E stat} / \_\_ ^{\#} \\ \text{E act} \end{cases}$

3. $\text{E stat} \rightarrow \begin{cases} \text{In E stat} / ^{\#} \_\_ \\ \text{In E stat}^{-1} \end{cases}$

4. $CCL \rightarrow \begin{cases} CF / \text{In E stat} + \_\_ \\ CF + CF \end{cases}$

5. $CF \longrightarrow \begin{cases} CF_t / \_\_ + ... + \text{In E stat}^{-1} \\ CF_c \end{cases}$

6. $\text{In E stat} \rightarrow \text{S stat}$

7. $\text{E act} \rightarrow \text{S act}$

8. $\text{In E stat}^{-1} \rightarrow \text{S stat}^{-1}$

9. $CF_t \rightarrow CT_t$

10. $CF_c \rightarrow CT_c$

11. $\text{S stat} \rightarrow \begin{cases} \textit{John was happy} \\ \textit{John was rich} \\ \textit{John was unhappy} \\ \textit{etc.} \end{cases}$

12. $\text{S act} \rightarrow \begin{cases} \textit{John met a woman} \\ \textit{John lost a lot of money} \\ \textit{etc.} \end{cases}$

$$13.\ \text{S stat}^{-1} \rightarrow \left\{ \begin{array}{l} \textit{John was unhappy / John was happy} + ... + -- \\ \textit{John was poor / John was rich} + ... + -- \\ \textit{John was happy / John was unhappy} + ... + -- \\ \textit{etc.} \end{array} \right\}$$

14. $CT_t \rightarrow$ *then*

15. $CT_c \rightarrow$ *as a result.*[22]

Suppose we apply these rules, we get a derivation of minimal story

(76) *John was happy, then John met a woman, then, as a result, John was unhappy.*

The number at the left of each line of the derivation refers to the rule of grammar used in constructing that line from each preceding line.

(77) M St

E + CCL + E + CCL + E	(1)
E stat + CCL + E + CCL + E	(2)
E stat + CCL + E + CCL + E stat	(2)
E stat + CCL + E act + CCL + E stat	(2)
In E stat + CCL + E act + CCL + E stat	(3)
In E stat + CCL + E act + CCL + In E stat^{-1}	(3)
In E stat + CF + E act + CCL + In E stat^{-1}	(4)
In E stat + CF + E act + CF + CF + In E stat^{-1}	(4)
In E stat + CF$_t$ + E act + CF + CF + In E stat^{-1}	(5)
In E stat + CF$_t$ + E act + CF$_t$ + CF + In E stat^{-1}	(5)
In E stat + CF$_t$ + E act + CF$_t$ + CF$_c$ + In E stat^{-1}	(5)
S stat + CF$_t$ + E act + CF$_t$ + CF$_c$ + In E stat^{-1}	(6)
S stat + CF$_t$ + S act + CF$_t$ + CF$_c$ + In E stat^{-1}	(7)
S stat + CF$_t$ + S act + CF$_t$ + CF$_c$ + S stat^{-1}	(8)
S stat + CT$_t$ + S act + CF$_t$ + CF$_c$ + S stat^{-1}	(9)
S stat + CT$_t$ + S act + CT$_t$ + CF$_c$ + S stat^{-1}	(9)
S stat + CT$_t$ + S act + CT$_t$ + CT$_c$ + S stat^{-1}	(10)
John was happy + CT$_t$ + S act + CT$_t$ + CT$_c$ + S stat^{-1}	(11)

---

[22]   Rules 6-15 are what may be called expression rules, i.e., rules describing how any given minimal story may be rendered through language.

John was happy + CT_t + *John met a woman* + CT_t + CT_c + S stat^{-1} (12)

John was happy + CT_t + *John met a woman* + CT_t + CT_c + *John was unhappy* (13)

John was happy + *then* + *John met a woman* + CT_t + CT_c + *John was unhappy* (14)

John was happy + *then* + *John met a woman* + *then* + CT_c + *John was unhappy* (14)

John was happy + *then* + *John met a woman* + *then* + *as a result* + *John was unhappy* (15)

We can represent derivation (77) by means of a tree diagram — no. (78) — which would not tell us in what order the rules were applied in (77) but would retain what is essential in (77) for the determination of the structure of minimal story (76).

Note that by applying rules 1-15 of the grammar, we could get not only the derivation of (76) but also the derivation of:

(79) *John was happy, then John lost a lot of money, then, as a result, John was unhappy*

(80) *John was rich, then John met a woman, then, as a result, John was poor*

(81) *John was rich, then John lost a lot of money, then, as a result, John was poor*

(82) *John was unhappy, then John met a woman, then, as a result, John was happy*

(83) *John was unhappy, then John lost a lot of money, then, as a result, John was happy.*

Each derivation could, of course, be represented by means of a tree diagram identical to (78) except for the terminal symbols: all minimal stories have the same structure.

Note also that, if in rules 11-13 S stat, S act and S stat^{-1} could be rewritten in x ways, we could get the derivation of x^2 minimal stories. As a matter of fact, appropriate expression rules would

(78)

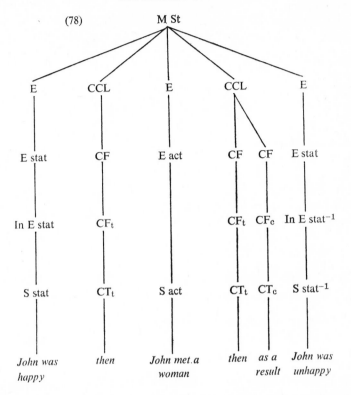

allow us to get the derivation of all minimal stories and only minimal stories.

2. THE KERNEL SIMPLE STORY

2.0 Every minimal story is a story but the reverse is not true. Consider the following examples:

(1) *John was rich, then John was poor, then he worked very hard, then, as a result, he was rich*

(2) *John was happy and John was rich and John was handsome, then he met a woman, then, as a result, he was unhappy*

(3) *The sun was shining and the birds were singing and the cotton was high and John was happy. Then, the sun set. Then, as a result, John was unhappy*

(4) *John was happy but then the army drafted him, then, as a result, he was unhappy*

(5) *John loved Mary but then he met Joan, then, as a result, he hated Mary*

(1)-(5) constitute stories. However, they are not minimal stories since four events are represented in (1), five are represented in (2), six are represented in (3), and since the events represented in (4) as well as those represented in (5) are conjoined by four conjunctive features.

(1)-(5) each contain a minimal story. In (1)-(5) we find (6)-(10) respectively:

(6) *John was poor, then he worked very hard, then, as a result, he was rich*

(7) *John was happy, then he met a woman, then, as a result, he was unhappy*

(8) *John was happy, then the sun set, then, as a result, John was unhappy*

(9) *John was happy, then the army drafted him, then, as a result, he was unhappy*

(10) *John loved Mary, then he met Joan, then, as a result, he hated Mary.*

On the other hand, (1)-(5) do not contain more than one minimal story (for instance two) whereas (11) and (12) do:

(11) *John was rich and Joan was poor. Then Joan made a lot of money, then, as a result, she was rich. Then John lost a lot of money, then, as a result, he was poor*

(12) *John loved Joan. Joan was very pretty, then she had a terrible accident, then, as a result, she was very ugly. Then John found out that Joan had become ugly, then, as a result, he hated her.*[1]

(1)-(5) also have at least one other feature in common. If I take, from now on, any series of events to be spatio-chronologically ordered whenever no event in that series preceding in time another event is placed after that event, then the events in (1)-(5) respectively are in spatio-chronological order. The events in (13) and (14), however, are not:

(13) *John met a woman, then, as a result, he was very unhappy. He had been very happy before*

(14) *John ate a magical apple, then, as a result, he was very rich. He had been very poor before.*[2]

I shall call *kernel simple story* any story the events of which are in spatio-chronological order and which contains no more than one

---

[1] For a discussion of stories containing more than one minimal story, see chapter IV.

[2] For a discussion of stories in which events are not in spatio-chronological order see chapter III.

minimal story. According to this definition, (1)-(5) are kernel simple stories and so are (6)-(10).

2.1 A minimal story consists of three conjoined events and a kernel simple story cannot therefore consist of less than three conjoined events. If there is thus a lower limit imposed on the number of events required to constitute a kernel simple story, is there an upper limit? Consider the following kernel simple story:

(15) *The birds were flying and the fish were swimming and John was happy. Then he saw a dead tree, then, as a result, he was unhappy.*

Suppose that preceding the first event in (15) — *The birds were flying* — we introduced a series of n events conjoined by *and*, the nth event being conjoined with *The birds were flying* by *and*. We would have for instance:

(16) *The sun was shining and the flowers were beautiful and ... and nth event and the birds were flying and the fish were swimming and John was happy. Then he saw a dead tree, then, as a result, he was unhappy.*

(16) would constitute a kernel simple story for its n events would be in spatio-chronological order and it would not contain more than one minimal story. A kernel simple story can therefore consist of n conjoined events, where n $\geq$ 3.

2.1.1 Of the n conjoined events constituting a kernel simple story, three and only three constitute a minimal story. These I will call *narrative* events. In (16) for instance,

(17) *John was happy*

(18) *He saw a dead tree*

(19) *He was unhappy*

are narrative events whereas all the other events are not.

The ratio of narrative and non-narrative events in a given story is of course very important since it affects its degree of narrativity. Consider, for instance, the following:

(20) *John was rich and he was happy, then he met a woman, then, as a result, he was unhappy*

(21) *John was rich and he was handsome and he was intelligent and he was happy. On the other hand, Mary was poor and she was ugly and she was stupid and she was unhappy. One day, John met Mary, then, as a result, he was unhappy.*

(20) which consists of four conjoined events, three of which are narrative, has a higher degree of narrativity than (21) which consists of ten conjoined events, three of which are narrative. Some stories have such a low degree of narrativity that they are difficult to recognize as stories. On the other hand, minimal stories for instance, though usually quite trivial, have the highest degree of narrativity possible.

2.1.2   If a kernel simple story can have n conjoined stative events as in (16), it can also have n conjoined active events as in:

(22) *John ate a banana, then he ate a pear, then ..., then nth active event, and he was happy. Then he got sick, then, as a result, he was unhappy.*

In a kernel simple story, n stative or active events may precede in time the first narrative event as in:

(23) *The sun rose, then the birds sang, then ..., then nth event. Then John went out and he felt very happy. Then he met Mary, then, as a result, he felt very unhappy*

or may follow in time the last narrative event as in:

(24) *John was very happy, then he met Mary, then, as a result, he was very unhappy. Then he ate a frankfurter, then he ate another frankfurter, then ..., then nth event*

or again may follow in time the first narrative event while preceding in time the second:

(25) *John was very happy, then he ate a frankfurter, then he ate
another frankfurter, then ..., then nth event. Then he met Mary,
then, as a result, he was very unhappy.*

However, no event may follow in time the second narrative event
while preceding in time the third: since the second narrative event
causes the third, if it occurs during a time terminating at instant
I then the third occurs during a time beginning at instant I.[3]

Moreover, I will now impose further restrictions on kernel simple
stories. If n events occur at the same time as the first narrative
event, they may appear before it, as in (16), or after it, as in:

(26) *John was happy and the sun was shining and the birds were
singing and ... and nth event. Then he saw Mary, then, as a
result, he was unhappy.*

or some may appear before it and some after it:

(27) *The sun was shining and the birds were singing and ... and
John was happy and the whole world was beautiful and ... and
nth event. Then John saw Mary, then, as a result, he was
unhappy.*

However, if n events occur at the same time as the second narrative
event, they may only appear before it and if n events occur at the
same time as the last narrative event they may only appear after
it. Thus,

(28) *John was very unhappy. The only thing that could make him
happy was to see a dead pigeon. One day, he heard a sparrow
and saw a dead pigeon. Then, as a result, he was very happy*

and

(29) *John was unhappy, then he met Mary, then, as a result, he
was happy though it was hot and it was raining*

would constitute kernel simple stories, whereas:

(30) *John was very unhappy. The only thing that could make him*

---

[3] I follow here C. J. Ducasse, *Truth, Knowledge and Causation* (London,
1968).

happy was to see a dead pigeon. One day, he saw a dead pigeon and heard a sparrow. Then, as a result, he was very happy

and

(31) *John was unhappy, then he met Mary, then as a result, though it was hot and it was raining, he was happy*

would not.

2.1.2.1 In any story there can be n active and n stative events. The proportion of active and stative events in a story clearly constitutes an important characteristic of that story. It is obvious, for instance, that a story in which most events are stative is much more static, much less dynamic, than one in which most events are active. Realistic novels, where detailed descriptions of situations and characters abound, and romantic novels, where local color is important and fifty pages or more can be devoted to the depiction of Constantinople or Notre-Dame, are more static than adventure stories, where descriptions are kept to a minimum and it is mainly the actions of various characters that matter. Similarly, modern mystery novels à la Mickey Spillane are more dynamic than classical detective stories à la Agatha Christie or S. S. Van Dine.

Furthermore, the distributional pattern of stative and active events in a given story or set of stories no doubt helps distinguish it from other stories or sets of stories. In some stories, a balance between stative and active events is maintained throughout. In other stories, on the contrary, stative, or active, events clearly predominate in certain sections. In many novels, for instance, the initial section differs from most if not all other sections in at least one way: it is largely made up of conjoined stative events because it is devoted to exposition, to giving the reader background information concerning the characters and the environment in which they live. Sometimes, the expository section of a novel can even make up an inordinately large part of that novel, as in some of Balzac's works. The following sections then seem tremendously dynamic by contrast. Of course, some novels, for instance Sartre's *L'Age de raison*, do not have any expository section.

2.2.0 No more than one conjunctive feature is needed to conjoin two events, no more than two are needed to conjoin three events, no more than three to conjoin four events, and no more than n-1 to conjoin n events. Since at least once in the course of a story two events must be conjoined by two conjunctive features rather than one — the first indicating that the events are in chronological order and the second that one event causes the other — we may say that in a kernel simple story consisting of n conjoined events we find at least n conjunctive features.

In a minimal story there are only two kinds of conjunctive features, one pointing out that the three events are in chronological order and the other that the second event causes the third. In a kernel simple story, it is of course possible to find more than two kinds of conjunctive features. Thus, in kernel simple stories

(32) *John was young but he was unhappy, then he met a woman,*
     then, as a result, he was happy

and

(33) *John was happy though he was poor, then he met a woman,*
     then, as a result, he was unhappy

the first conjunctive feature does not indicate that the first and second event are in chronological order nor that the first event causes the second.

Indeed, it is possible to find in a kernel simple story any conjunctive feature not implying that two events are conjoined in a way that contradicts spatio-chronological order. In given kernel simple stories we may find, for instance:

(34) *John was young and he was unhappy*

(35) *John was unhappy therefore he was nasty*

(36) *John was unhappy though he was rich*

(37) *John was young but he was poor*

(38) *John was rich then he was poor*

(39) *John was happy when he was drunk*

but not

(40) *John ate an apple after he drank the wine*

since in (40) a conjunctive feature conjoins two events in a way contradicting spatio-chronological order.

2.2.0.1   In a minimal story, the causal relationship between two events must be accompanied by a chronological one (see 1.2.2.2). The same is not true of the kernel simple story, where two events conjoined only causally may appear:

(41) *John was a professor therefore he was a fool*

(42) *John was intelligent because he was French.*

2.2.1   In a kernel simple story, some conjunctive features indicate that two conjoined events belong to different time sequences:

(43) *John ate a banana then he ate a pear*

while others indicate that two conjoined events belong to the same time sequence:

(44) *John was young and he was handsome.*

Any group of conjoined events belonging to the same time sequence constitutes an episode. There are four events but only three episodes in

(45) *John was happy and he was rich, then he met a woman, then, as a result, he was unhappy*

and there are six events and four episodes in

(46) *John was happy and he was rich and he was handsome, then he met a woman, then he was humiliated by her, then, as a result, he was unhappy.*

We may say therefore that a kernel simple story consists of n conjoined episodes, where n $\geqslant$ 3 and where any episode consists of one or more events.

Any episode containing a narrative event is a narrative episode. In (46),

(47) *John was happy and he was rich and he was handsome*

constitutes a narrative episode whereas

(48) *he met a woman*

does not. Obviously, in a kernel simple story, n episodes may precede in time the first narrative episode, or follow in time the last narrative episode, or again follow in time the first narrative episode while preceding in time the second; no episode, however, may follow in time the second narrative episode while preceding in time the third. Furthermore, no event may appear after the narrative event of the second narrative episode or before the narrative event of the third narrative episode (see 2.1.2).

2.2.1.1 It is relatively easy to determine the number of episodes in a story. In any story, events belong to different episodes if "their order cannot be changed without changing the inferred sequence of events in the original semantic interpretation".[4] On the other hand, events are part of the same episode if their order can be changed without changing the inferred sequence of events in the original semantic interpretation. Thus there are two episodes in:

(49) *He ate an apple then he ate a pear*

and

(50) *John saw Mary and fell*

whereas there is only one episode in:

(51) *John was happy and he was handsome*

(52) *Mary was nice and she was rich and she was young*

(53) *He ate a lot but he drank very little.*[5]

---

[4]   William Labov and Joshua Waletzky, "Narrative Analysis. Oral Versions of Personal Experience", *Essays on the Verbal and Visual Arts. Proceedings of the Annual Spring Meeting of the American Ethnological Society* (1966), 21.
[5]   For a detailed study of temporal sequence in stories and, more generally,

2.2.1.2 The proportion of episodes and events in a story is clearly one of the factors determining the pace at which that story unfolds in time. The greater the proportion of episodes, the more quickly the story moves forward. Moreover, by changing the proportion of episodes and events at various points in a given story, a storyteller would be capable of giving that story a specific rhythm and of underlining the importance of some passages rather than others.

2.2.1.3 Conjoined events constituting an episode must be all stative or all active:

(54) *John was happy and he was handsome*

(55) *John ate an apple and Bill ate a pear.*

Given two conjoined events one of which is stative and the other active, we would then be in the presence of two episodes:

(56) *John was sleeping when Bill came in*

(57) *John was eating but Mary interrupted him.*

In (56) as well as (57), the beginning of the first event precedes in time the beginning of the second. The first and second events therefore belong to different time sequences, to different episodes.

2.2.2 In a minimal story, there is only one cluster of conjunctive features. In a kernel simple story, there can be n such clusters, where $n \geq 1$. Thus, in

(58) *John was rich but then he lost a lot of money, then, as a result, he was poor*

and

(59) *John was happy but then he became sad. But then he met Mary, then, as a result, he was happy again*

there are two and three clusters respectively.

---

in narratives, see Labov and Waletzky, "Narrative Analysis. Oral Versions of Personal Experience", 12-44. See also Hristo Todorov, "Logique et temps narratif", *Information sur les Sciences Sociales*, VII, no. 6 (1968), 41-49.

The proportion of clusters of conjunctive features in a story is one of the main factors contributing to the uniqueness of that story. All other things being equal, a story containing five clusters would achieve more cohesiveness than one containing two clusters:

(60) *John was sad, then he made a lot of money, then, as a result, he met Bill, then, as a result, he went to Germany, then, as a result, he had many adventures, then, as a result, he met Mary, then, as a result, he was happy*

is more cohesive than

(61) *John was sad, then he made a lot of money, then he met Bill, then he went to Germany, then he had many adventures, then, as a result, he met Mary, then, as a result, he was happy.*

This was noticed long ago by Aristotle, who made a distinction between dramatic plot (i.e., unified or closely knit) and epic plot (i.e., loosely woven).

The distribution of clusters of conjunctive features in a story is also important. Certain distributional patterns can give parts of a story more cohesiveness than others. Suppose a storyteller wants to indicate that the life of his hero starts by being meaningless, then progressively becomes more and more meaningful. He may do it partially by avoiding clusters at first, then gradually introducing more and more of them. Similarly, certain distributional patterns of clusters can make the various episodes of a story very cohesive in themselves but barely conjoined with one another. This is the case in the epic or in the picaresque novel, where the protagonist goes from one adventure to another one with which it is barely connected.

Of course, the kinds of conjunctive features and clusters of conjunctive features found in a story constitute still another characteristic of that story and provide a useful tool for the classification of stories. In picaresque narratives, conjunctive features indicating a chronological relationship between events are numerous. The nineteenth century, with the novels of such writers as

Balzac, Meredith, and James, is the age in which logical relationships between events abound. And in the twentieth century conjunctive features which allow the storyteller to unfold his creation not temporally or logically but associationally have reached an unusual prominence, for instance in the novels of Virginia Woolf.

2.3 The grammar established in 1.4 can account for the structure of minimal stories but not for the structure of kernel simple stories. However, with the addition of certain rules to it and the modification of certain others, a new grammar can be constituted accounting for the structure of all and only kernel simple stories. Like the grammar of minimal stories, this grammar will consist of a set of symbols interrelated by an ordered set of rules, each rule being of the form $X \rightarrow Y$ and obeying restrictions (a)-(d) in 1.3, and only one rule being applied at a time.

The addition and/or modification of rules entails the introduction of several new symbols, such as:

N ep   = narrative episode
ep   = episode
Ne stat = narrative stative event
Ne act = narrative active event

and so on.

2.4 The rules constituting the grammar of kernel simple stories are the following:

1. St $\rightarrow$ N Sec + CCL + N Sec + CCL + N Sec
2. N Sec $\rightarrow$ $\begin{cases} \text{N ep (CCL + Ep) } / \text{ --- } \# \\ \text{(Ep + CCL) N ep} \end{cases}$
3. Ep $\rightarrow$ ep (CCL + Ep')
4. Ep' $\rightarrow$ Ep
5. CCL $\rightarrow$ $\begin{cases} CF_t + \text{sub CCL} / ... + \text{N ep} + ... + \text{N ep} + \text{---} \\ CF_t \text{ (sub CCL)} \end{cases}$

6. $N \ ep \rightarrow$
$$\begin{cases} \text{(E stat + sub CCL) Ne stat (sub CCL + E stat) /} \\ -- + ... + \text{N ep} + ... + \text{N ep} \\ \text{Ne stat (sub CCL + E stat) / Ne stat} + ... + -- \\ \text{(E act + sub CCL) Ne act} \end{cases}$$

7. $ep \rightarrow \begin{cases} \text{E stat} \\ \text{E act} \end{cases}$

8. E stat $\rightarrow$ e stat (sub CCL + E' stat)

9. E' stat $\rightarrow$ E stat

10. E act $\rightarrow$ e act (sub CCL + E' act)

11. E' act $\rightarrow$ E act

12. Ne stat $\rightarrow \begin{cases} \text{In Ne stat /} -- + ... + \text{Ne stat} \\ \text{In Ne stat}^{-1} \end{cases}$

13. sub CCL $\rightarrow \begin{cases} \text{CF}_c \ (\text{CF}_n) / -- + \text{In Ne stat}^{-1} \\ (\text{CF}_c) \ \text{CF}_n \\ \text{CF}_c \end{cases}$

14. e stat $\rightarrow$ S stat

15. e act $\rightarrow$ S act

16. In Ne stat $\rightarrow$ NS stat

17. Ne act $\rightarrow$ S act

18. In Ne stat^{-1} $\rightarrow$ NS stat^{-1}

19. $\text{CF}_t \rightarrow \text{CT}_t$

20. $\text{CF}_c \rightarrow \text{CT}_c$

21. $\text{CF}_n \rightarrow \text{CT}_n$

22. NS stat $\longrightarrow \begin{cases} \textit{John was happy} \\ \textit{John was unhappy} \\ \textit{etc.} \end{cases}$

23. NS stat^{-1} $\rightarrow \begin{cases} \textit{John was unhappy / John was happy} +...+ -- \\ \textit{John was happy / John was unhappy} +...+ -- \\ \textit{etc.} \end{cases}$

24. S stat $\longrightarrow \begin{cases} \textit{the sun was shining} \\ \textit{the birds were singing} \\ \textit{John was rich} \\ \textit{etc.} \end{cases}$

25. S act $\longrightarrow$ $\left\{\begin{array}{l} \textit{John met a woman} \\ \textit{John met Bill} \\ \textit{John met Mary} \\ \textit{etc.} \end{array}\right\}$

26. $CT_t \rightarrow then$

27. $CT_c \rightarrow as\ a\ result$

28. $CT_n \rightarrow$ $\left\{\begin{array}{l} \textit{however} \\ \textit{though} \\ \textit{and} \\ \textit{etc.} \end{array}\right\}$[6]

[6] Rules 3-4 and 8-11 indicate perhaps far too much structure for the simple conjunction of episodes or events. For instance,

(62) *John was happy and the sun was shining and the birds were singing*

would be represented by the (simplified) tree diagram on the next page.

To provide for a simpler structure, we may modify our rules and introduce transformational rules (see 3.5 and 4.4) which would allow for the conjunction of n episodes or events. If rules 8-9, for instance, were replaced by a rule

E stat $\rightarrow$ e stat (sub CCL + e stat)

and a transformational rule

SA: of (a): e stat + sub CCL + e stat
of (b): e stat + sub CCL + e stat
SC: (1-2-3; 4-5-6) $\rightarrow$ 1-2-3-5-6
(where 3=4)

were introduced, the new rules would allow us to obtain (62); (I am grossly simplifying). Another way to provide for a simpler structure would be to consider, by analogy with string analysis, an episode or event to be the center of a string composed of a sequence of episodes or events. The other episodes or events in the string would then be regarded as adjuncts to the center. (On the subject of string analysis, see Zellig Harris, *String Analysis of Sentence Structure* (The Hague, 1967). See also William O. Hendricks, "Linguistics and the structural Analysis of Literary Texts" and, by the same author, "On the Notion 'Beyond the Sentence'".) Both possibilities, however, raise several difficult problems and would considerably complicate our grammar.

A much more serious defect of the grammar is that it would assign identical structures to stories like

(63) *John was happy and the birds were singing and the sun was shining, then John met Mary, then, as a result, he was unhappy*

and

If we apply these rules we get a derivation of kernel simple story

(65) *The sun was shining and the birds were singing and John was
     happy, then John met Bill, then, as a result, John met Mary,
     then, as a result, John was unhappy.*

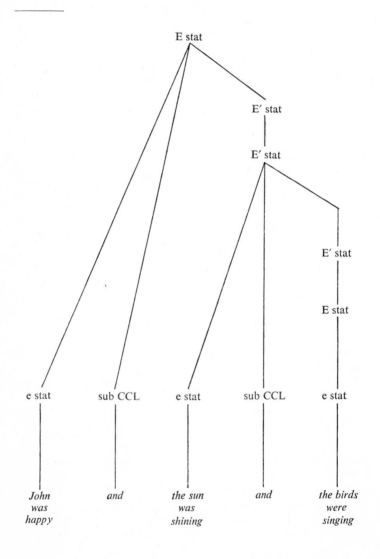

The derivation could be represented by diagram (66), which retains what is essential in it for the determination of the structure of (65).

Note that by applying rules 1-28 of the grammar, we could get not only the derivation of (65) but also that of:

(67) *John was happy, then John met Bill, then, as a result, John met Mary, then, as a result, John was unhappy and the sun was shining and the birds were singing*

(68) *John was unhappy and the sun was shining and the birds were singing, then John met Bill, then, as a result, John met Mary, then, as a result, John was happy*

(69) *John was unhappy, then John met Bill, then John met Mary, then, as a result, John was happy*

and so on and so forth. The various derivations could, of course, be represented by means of tree diagrams different from one another and from (66): (65), (67), (68) and (69) have different structures.

Note also that the application of rules 1-28 would yield minimal story (74) in 1.4, represented by the tree diagram (70).

Finally, note that although rules 1-28 cannot by themselves account for the structure of all stories since they cannot account for the structure of non-kernel simple stories, they will be used, along with another set of rules, to account for the structure of non-kernel simple stories: rules 1-28 constitute a fundamental component of my grammar of stories, a component that I will call *grammar G* from now on.

---

(64) *John was happy and the birds were singing because the sun was shining, then John met Mary, then, as a result, he was unhappy.*

Once again, a solution may perhaps be arrived at by modifying certain rewrite rules and introducing transformational rules or by using a method analogous to string analysis.

(66)

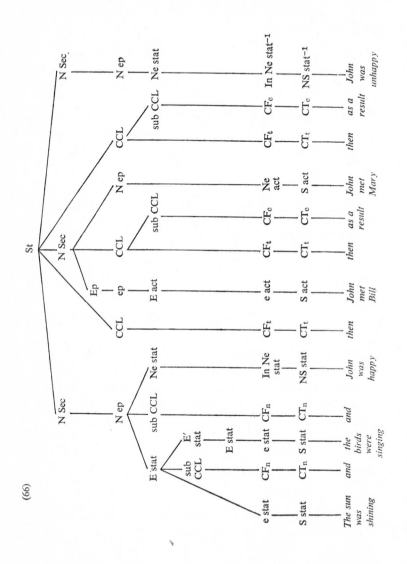

(70)

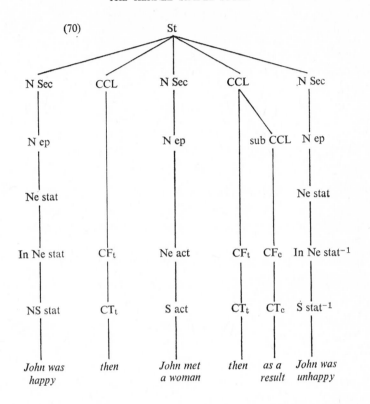

3. THE SIMPLE STORY

3.0 Grammar G can describe the structure of many stories but is incapable of describing that of many others. In particular, if it can account for the structure of a kernel simple story A, there are paraphrases of A for which it cannot account. Thus, grammar G would yield the structure of the following stories:

(1) *John had been happy, then John met Mary, then, as a result, John was unhappy*

(2) *John had been rich, then John was poor, then John worked very hard, then, as a result, John was rich*

(3) *The sun was shining and John was happy, then the sun set, then, as a result, John was unhappy*

(4) *Once upon a time, falling in love cured sickness. At that time, John was rich but he was sick. He tried many cures but did not recover his health. Then he fell in love with Mary, then, as a result, he was healthy*

(5) *John was poor, then his uncle died, then, as a result, John inherited a fortune, then, as a result, John was rich*

(6) *John was happy. Then his wife gave birth to a beautiful baby and his mother died. Then, as a result, John was unhappy.*

On the other hand, grammar G would not yield the structure of (7)-(12) which paraphrase (1)-(6) respectively:

(7) *John met Mary, then, as a result, John was unhappy. Before John met Mary, John had been happy*

(8) *John was poor. Before he was poor, John had been rich. After he was poor, John worked very hard, then, as a result, John was rich*

(9) *The sun was shining and John was happy. Then John was unhappy because the sun set*

(10) *Once upon a time, falling in love cured sickness. At that time, John was rich but he was sick. He tried many cures but did not recover his health. Then he fell in love with Mary*

(11) *John was poor, then his uncle died, then, as a result, John inherited a fortune*

(12) *John was happy. Then his mother died and his wife gave birth to a beautiful baby. Then, as a result of his mother's death, John was unhappy.*

3.1 The fundamental difference between (1)-(2) on the one hand and (7)-(8) on the other is that whereas, in the former, events are in chronological order, in the latter, they are not. To put it a little differently, what may be called story order is identical with chronological order in (1)-(2) but not in (7)-(8).[1]

3.1.1 Story order and chronological order often do not coincide. Thus, one of the favorite devices of storytellers is the flashback: through an associative process breaking up chronological sequence, a series of events having occurred in the past is telescoped into a series of events occurring in the present. Another popular device breaking up chronological sequence is the flash-forward, which may be defined as the opposite of the flashback. By using flashbacks and flash-forwards, and more generally by not presenting events in their chronological sequence, a storyteller is not only able to draw striking parallels between different situations or to reveal the future of his protagonists for purposes of irony, but he is also able to vary the mode of development of his story. One of the major

[1] On various differences between story order and chronological order, see, among others, Tzvetan Todorov, *Théorie de la littérature*, 263-307.

reasons for the uniqueness of *A la recherche du temps perdu* is the unorthodox way in which Proust's masterpiece unfolds: it is entirely organized around a series of subtly distributed flashbacks and flash-forwards.

The relationship between story order and chronological order provides a tool for the classification of various sets of stories. Tzvetan Todorov, for instance, uses that relationship to distinguish between the two fundamental types of detective story, the "roman à mystère" and the "roman d'aventures":

> Dans le premier cas, l'histoire est donnée dès les premières pages, mais elle est incompréhensible: un crime est accompli presque sous nos yeux mais nous n'en avons pas connu les véritables agents ni les vrais mobiles. L'enquête consiste à revenir sans cesse sur les mêmes événements, à vérifier et corriger les moindres détails, jusqu'à ce qu'à la fin éclate la vérité sur cette même histoire initiale. Dans l'autre cas, pas de mystère, pas de retour en arrière: chaque événement en provoque un autre et l'intérêt que nous portons à l'histoire ne vient pas d'une révélation sur les données initiales; c'est celle de leurs conséquences qui maintient le suspense.[2]

3.1.2 The way story order differs from chronological order is often related to some extent to the goals of the storyteller. Thus, if a storyteller wishes to eliminate all suspense from his tale in order to better focus the interest of his audience on aspects other than plot, he may reveal the outcome of his story well before the events leading up to it. If, on the contrary, a storyteller wishes to frustrate his audience, for one reason or another, he may constantly introduce events which, instead of moving his story forward to its conclusion, move it in the opposite direction. This is a technique favored in many anti-novels, for example John Barth's *The Floating Opera*.

3.1.3 The degree of difference between story order and chronological order seems to be considerably affected by the medium through which a story is expressed. Oral narratives break up the

---

[2] Tzvetan Todorov, "La Quête du récit", 208-209. See also Tzvetan Todorov, "Les Catégories du récit littéraire", 140.

chronological sequence of events much less often than written narratives, probably because it would otherwise be very difficult for their audience to follow their development.[3] Similarly, stories told by means of moving pictures keep much closer to chronological sequence than stories expressed through written language probably because it is quite cumbersome in a movie to go back and forth in time and because it is rather difficult for an audience, especially an unsophisticated one, to distinguish between, say, flashbacks and flash-forwards.[4] It is interesting to note that, whereas the flashback has long been a popular cinematic technique, the flash-forward was introduced in movies only recently and, in my opinion, not very successfully.[5]

3.1.3.1 Notice that, in a story expressed through language, it is very difficult to present events in a strictly chronological order. As Tzvetan Todorov puts it:

Dans l'histoire, plusieurs événements peuvent se dérouler en même temps; mais le discours doit obligatoirement les mettre à la suite l'un de l'autre; une figure complexe se trouve projetée sur une ligne droite. C'est de là que vient la nécessité de rompre la succession 'naturelle' des événements même si l'auteur voulait la suivre au plus près.[6]

Because it is impossible to render through language simultaneous events simultaneously, a storyteller must explicitly say that events expressed one after the other are in reality cotemporaneous or must give that impression. Sometimes the results can be strikingly effective. In the twentieth century, the so-called technique of simultaneism has been successfully used several times, for instance in Dos Passos' *1919*, Jules Romains' *Le Drapeau noir*, and Sartre's *Le Sursis*.

---

[3] Note that early written narratives break up chronological sequence rather rarely because they are still close to oral tradition.
[4] Unless, of course, specific dates are assigned to various scenes, for instance by means of a calendar.
[5] The flash-forward definitely fails in movies like *Petulia* or *They Shoot Horses, Don't They?*
[6] Tzvetan Todorov, "Les Catégories du récit littéraire", 139.

3.2 The difference between (3) and (9) above is twofold. If, in (3), story order and chronological order are identical, in (9) they are not. Furthermore, in (3) the third event causes the fourth whereas in (9) the reverse is true.

Like the relationship between story order and chronological order, the way causes and their results are ordered constitutes an important feature of various sets of stories. Generally speaking, for instance, in stories which study primarily the psychological makeup of a character, one of his states of mind is often described first, then a series of events explain what this state of mind is the result of. In adventure stories, on the other hand, the consequence of a series of events is usually not described before that series of events.

3.3 The difference between (4)-(5) and (10)-(11) above is in no way related to the order of events: in all four stories, the events are ordered spatio-chronologically and no consequence of a given event is made to appear before that event. Rather, the difference is that in (10)

(13) *Then, as a result, he was healthy*

is not expressed whereas it is expressed in (4). Similarly, in (11)

(14) *Then, as a result, John was rich*

is not expressed whereas it is expressed in (5). From now on, I shall call any event which is not expressed a *zeroed* event. Any cluster of conjunctive features conjoining a zeroed event with the event preceding it is also zeroed.

If one studies (10) and (11), the zeroed event in each is easily retrievable. (10) explains that falling in love cures sickness. To understand that John became healthy after being sick, it is therefore enough to know that he fell in love. Similarly, it is not necessary for two events to be expressed in (11), one indicating that John inherited a fortune and the other that, as a result, John was rich: knowing that John inherited a fortune is enough to understand that he became rich. Like (13) and (14), any event in a story may be zeroed if and only if it is retrievable on the basis of an examination of the remainder of the story and it is not presupposed by another event in the story.

In a given story, therefore, at least some events may not be zeroed. Consider the following story:

(15) *Eating pizza leads to evil. John was good, then, one day, he ate pizza, then, as a result, he was evil.*

The last event may be zeroed (along with the cluster of conjunctive features conjoining it with the preceding event) because

(16) *Then, as a result, he was evil*

can be retrieved from

(17) *Eating pizza leads to evil. John was good, then, one day, he ate pizza.*

On the other hand, the next to last event (along with the conjunctive feature conjoining it with the preceding event) may not be zeroed because

(18) *Then, one day, he ate pizza*

cannot be retrieved from

(19) *Eating pizza leads to evil. John was good, then, as a result, he was evil.*

3.3.1   (10), (11), and (17) are examples of stories in which the last of three narrative events has been zeroed. There are many stories in which the first narrative event is zeroed. Consider, for instance

(20) *John inherited a fortune, then, as a result, he was very rich, then he met Mary, then, as a result, he was very poor*

and

(21) *John inherited a fortune, then he met Mary, then, as a result, he was very poor.*

The main difference between (20) and (21) is that the first narrative event

(22) *He was very rich*

has been zeroed in (21), along with, of course, the cluster of conjunctive features conjoining it with the preceding event, but it has not been zeroed in (20).

3.3.2 If we examine (10), we find that it is one event in particular, the first one, which allows for the zeroing of (13). Similarly, when we study (11), we find that it is one event in particular, the last one, which allows for the zeroing of (14). (10) and (11) are very short stories. In longer stories, there often are many events or series of events allowing for the zeroing of other events. Such events, along with other elements in a story contributing to the understanding of that story, are code units and together they constitute the code of the story.

Any story has a code and it is not unduly difficult to isolate it. Consider a novel like *Billion Dollar Brain*, for instance. At the very beginning of it, the narrator-protagonist is on his way to his office: "Behind me I heard Alice puffing up the stairs with a catering size tin of Nescafé. Someone in the dispatch department put a brass-band record on the gramophone. Dawlish, my boss, was always complaining about that gramophone ...".[7] He seems simply to be recording for himself what he heard and thought. Yet, there is at least one bit of information in this passage functioning as a code unit. The narrator has no reason to tell himself something which he knows perfectly well, namely, who Dawlish is. If he does, it is because he has to develop the code necessary to the understanding of his story. Similarly, in *Une Ténébreuse Affaire*, Balzac describes two women terrorized by a man, then adds: "L'aspect du mari pouvait expliquer jusqu'à un certain point la terreur des deux femmes. Les lois de la physionomie sont exactes, non seulement dans leur application au caractère, mais encore

---

[7] Len Deighton, *Billion Dollar Brain* (Middlesex: Penguin Books, 1966), 11.

relativement à la fatalité de l'existence ...".[8] The explanation of the women's terror is not intended for them and functions as a code unit. As a general rule, whenever a story provides such data, they constitute at least part of the code of that story.

The complexity and size of a story code varies a great deal from one set of stories to another. Usually, the code is both simple and minimal in adventure novels. These novels have a high degree of narrativity and relate events in a straightforward manner. On the other hand, the code is quite large and complex in the Balzacian and Proustian novels. In fact, these novels are often mainly composed of the motivations and justifications of certain events.[9]

3.4 In both (6) and (12) above, events are spatio-chronologically ordered. Furthermore, in both stories, no event has been zeroed. However, whereas in (6) the event occurring at the same time as the second narrative event appears before it, in (12) the event occurring at the same time as the second narrative event appears after it. As stated in 2.1.2, this means that (6) is a kernel simple story while (12) is not.

3.5 Though (1)-(6) constitute kernel simple stories and (7)-(12) do not, they all have at least one characteristic in common. (1)-(12) each contain no more than one minimal story. Any story which contains no more than one minimal story is a *simple story*.[10]

In order to account for simple stories like (7)-(12), it is necessary to add a new set of rules to grammar G. These rules will be transformational and will allow us to perform certain changes in certain strings, provided these strings have a certain structure.[11] The first

[8] Balzac, *Une Ténébreuse Affaire* (Paris: Le Livre de Poche, 1963), 17.

[9] On the question of story codes, see Barthes, "Introduction à l'analyse structurale des récits", 1-27, Gérard Genette, "Vraisemblable et motivation", *Communications*, no. 11 (1968), 5-21, and Gerald Prince, "On Readers and Listeners in Narrative", *Neophilologus*. LV, no. 2 (1971), 117-122.

[10] Cf. Propp, *Morphology of the Folktale* and the one-move folktale.

[11] In my elaboration of transformational rules, I once again follow Noam Chomsky's *Syntactic Structures*; "On the Notion 'Rule of Grammar'"; "A Transformational Approach to Syntax"; and Emmon Bach, *An Introduction to Transformational Grammars*.

part of a transformational rule is a structural analysis specifying the kind of string (in terms of its structure) to which the rule applies. A transformational rule might apply for instance to all and only stories which can be analyzed as follows, according to grammar G:

SA: N ep – CF_t – ep – CF_t – Ne act – CF_t – CF_c – N ep

The structural analysis often contains symbols like X or Y, standing for any strings. Suppose only the three elements ep, CF_t and Ne act must be specified in the transformational rule, the structural analysis may be given as follows:

SA: X – ep – CF_t – Ne act – Y

The second part of the rule specifies the structural change by means of numbers referring to the segments specified by the structural analysis. Thus, given SA above, 1 would refer to X, 2 would refer to ep, 5 would refer to Y, and the structural change might be:

SC: 1– 2 – 3 – 4 – 5 → 1 – 4 – before 4 – 2 – 5

Note that sometimes it is necessary to describe certain conditions that must be met in addition to those specified in the structural analysis. Suppose, for instance, that, in a transformation applying to a string ep – CCL – ep – CCL – ep, it were necessary to specify that the two clusters of conjunctive features are not identical, we might add a condition:

(where 2 ≠ 4)

Note also that from now on I shall call transformational rules applying to a single string singulary transformations.

3.6   Simple stories such as (7) could be accounted for if we applied to a specific string yielded by grammar G the following rule:

Note that Julia Kristeva in "Problèmes de la structuration du texte", *La Nouvelle Critique*, no. spécial (1968), 55-64 and in "Narration et transformation", *Semiotica*, I, no. 4 (1969), 422-448 uses the notion of transformation in building a model of novels. However, she makes a gross mistake in equating deep structure with competence and surface structure with performance.

T_{1a} SA: X – Str ep – CF_t – Str ep – y
   SC: $1 - 2 - 3 - 4 - 5 \rightarrow 1 - 4 - \text{before} - 4 - 2 - 5$
      (where Str ep is any series of episodes and/or narrative
      episodes; 1 and 5 are null)

The rule shows that a series of episodes and/or narrative episodes
may appear after another series of episodes and/or narrative
episodes even though the first series precedes the second in time,
provided that no episode or narrative episode precedes the first
series or follows the second and that the constant *before* is
introduced to indicate the original order of the elements.

(1) and (7) may of course be represented by tree diagrams making clear the difference between them. (1) would be represented
by diagram (23).

(23)

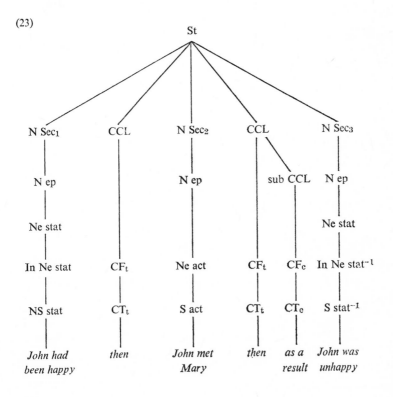

Applying T_{1a} to (23) would yield (7), which would be represented by diagram (24).

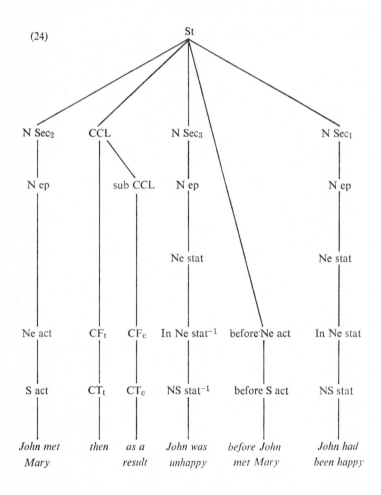

(24)

It is clear that T_{1a} would not help account for the structure of (8) and similar stories. However, when applied to a specific string yielded by grammar **G**, the following rule would:

T_{1b} SA: X – Str ep – CF_t – Str ep – CF_t – Y

SC: 1 – 2 – 3 – 4 – 5 – 6 → 1 – 4 – before 4 – 2 – after 4 – 6
(where Str ep is any series of episodes and/or narrative
episodes; 6 is not null)

Note that T_{1b} is similar to T_{1a} and performs similar changes in
the structure of a given string. Note also that if (2) is represented
by diagram (25):

(25)

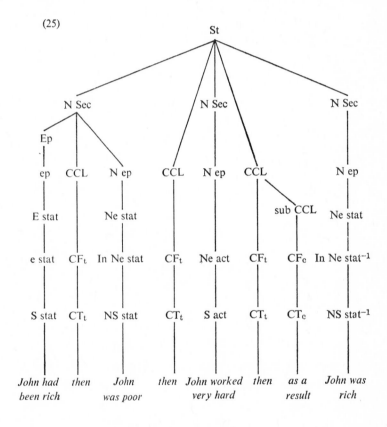

then applying T_{1b} to (25) would yield diagram (26) representing (8).

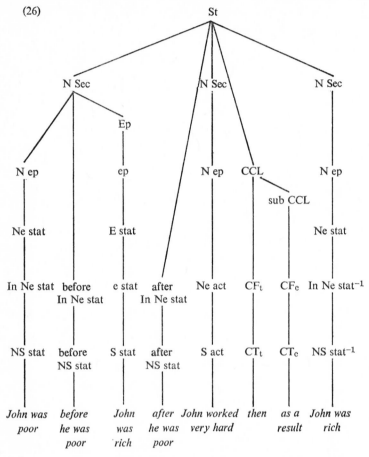

(26)

Other singulary transformations would help us account for the structure of other simple stories which are not kernel simple stories. Thus,

T_{2a}: SA: $X - CF_t - Ne\ act - CF_t - CF_c - In\ Ne\ stat^{-1}-Y$
  SC: $1 - 2 - 3 - 4 - 5 - 6 - 7 \rightarrow 1 - 2 - 6 - CF\ because -$
    before 6 after $1 - 7$
  (where 7 is null)

T_{3a}: SA: $X - CCL - Ne$ stat $- Y$

SC: $1 - 2 - 3 - 4 \rightarrow 1 - CCL_0 - Ne$ stat$_0 - 4$

(where 3 is retrievable from the remainder of the string; subscript 0 indicates that any symbol it is attached to represents an element not expressed in the story)

T_4: SA: $X - CF_t - e$ act $- CF_n - Ne$ act $- CF_t - CF_c - In$ Ne stat$^{-1} - Y$

SC: $1 - 2 - 3 - 4 - 5 - 6 - 7 - 8 - 9 \rightarrow 1 - 2 - 5 - 4 - 3 - 6 - CF_c$ of $4 - 8 - 9$

(where 1 is a string of episodes and/or narrative episodes: 9 is null)

would help assign a structure to 9-12.

Still other singular transformations, such as

T_{1c}: SA: $X - Str$ ev $- CF_n - Str$ ev $- CF_t - Str$ ep $- CCL - ep - CF_t - Str$ ep $- Y$

SC: $1 - 2 - 3 - 4 - 5 - 6 - 7 - 8 - 9 - 10 - 11 \rightarrow 1 - 2 - 5 - 6 - 7 - 8 - 3 -$ before 5 at the same time as $2 - 4 - 9 - 10 - 11$

(where Str ev is any series of events and/or narrative events; Str ep is any series of episodes and/or narrative episodes)

T_{2b}: SA: $X - Str$ ep $- CF_t - ep - CF_t - CF_c - ep - CF_t - Str$ ep $- Y$

SC: $1 - 2 - 3 - 4 - 5 - 6 - 7 - 8 - 9 - 10 \rightarrow 1 - 2 - 3 - 7 - CF$ because $-$ before 7 after $2 - 4 - 8 - 9 - 10$

T_{3b}: SA: $X - CCL - e$ stat $- Y$

SC: $1 - 2 - 3 - 4 \rightarrow 1 - CCL_0 - e$ stat$_0 - 4$

T_{3c}: SA: $X - $ sub $CCL - Ne$ stat $- Y$

SC: $1 - 2 - 3 - 4 \rightarrow 1 - $ sub $CCL_0 - Ne$ stat$_0 - 4$

would help us account for the structure of other simple stories.[12]

Thus far, I have shown that the structure of some simple stories can be accounted for by applying a single transformational rule

[12] I am giving T_{1a}-T_4 simply as possible examples of rules that would help account for the structure of simple stories which are not kernel simple stories. In a more thoroughly worked out grammar of stories, T_{1a}-T_4 would most probably have to be replaced by other singular transformations.

to a structure described by grammar G. There are stories the structure of which can be accounted for only through the use of more than one transformational rule. Transformational rules should therefore operate in such a way that they can apply not only to structures yielded by grammar G but also to structures that have already been transformed: moreover, the product of a transformation should be capable of undergoing further changes. For instance, the structure of

(27) *Bill died, then John inherited a fortune; before Bill died, John was poor*

would be accounted for by: a) applying T_{3a}; b) applying T_{1a} to the structure obtained after the application of T_{3a}. Of course, (27) is itself capable of undergoing further changes.[13]

In conclusion, note that, given grammar G and the appropriate singulary transformations, we could account for the structure of any simple story.

---

[13] Like the rules in grammar G, transformational rules probably have to be (partially) ordered. At this point, however, it is obviously not possible to determine the order in which transformations must apply.

4. THE COMPLEX STORY

4.0 Consider the following stories:

(1) *John was poor, then he found gold in his field, then, as a result, he was rich. Then, as a result, Peter was sad, then he found oil in his field, then, as a result, he was happy*

(2) *John was happy, then he met Joan, then, as a result, John was unhappy, then he met Mary, then, as a result, he was happy*

(3) *John was rich and Joan was happy, then John lost a lot of money, then, as a result, John was poor and Joan was unhappy*

(4) *John was happy and Joan was unhappy, then John got divorced and Joan got married, then, as a result, John was unhappy and Joan was happy*

(5) *John was rich and Joan was poor. Then Joan made money, then, as a result, she was rich. Then John lost money, then, as a result, he was poor*

(6) *John loved Joan. Joan was very pretty, then she had a terrible accident, then, as a result, she was very ugly. Then John saw Joan, then, as a result, he hated her.*

(1)-(6) have at least one feature in common. They all have more than three narrative events, or, to put it differently, they all contain more than one minimal story. For instance, (1) contains

(7) *John was poor, then he found gold in his field, then, as a result, he was rich*

and

(8) *Peter was sad, then he found oil in his field, then, as a result, he was happy*

and (3) contains

(9) *John was rich, then John lost a lot of money, then, as a result, John was poor*

and

(10) *Joan was happy, then John lost a lot of money, then, as a result, Joan was unhappy.*

(1)-(6) are therefore not simple stories (see 3.5) but rather combinations of simple stories. From now on, I shall call *complex story* any story containing more than one simple story[1] and I shall call *component story* any simple story which is part of a complex story.

4.1 Different combinational patterns of simple stories produce different kinds of complex stories. Scholars generally distinguish three fundamental types of combination: conjoining, alternation, and embedding.[2] In conjoining, a simple story may be conjoined with another story by means of a conjunctive feature or a cluster of conjunctive features. Thus, in (1), (7) is conjoined with (8) by means of *then, as a result*. As for (2), it is the product of a more particular case of conjoining. It is constituted by

(11) *John was happy, then he met Joan, then, as a result, John was unhappy*

(12) *John was unhappy, then he met Mary, then, as a result, he was happy*

and the last narrative event in (11) is identical with the first narrative event in (12).

---

[1] Cf. Propp, *Morphology of the Folktale* and the n-move folktale.

[2] See, among others, Claude Bremond, "La Logique des possibles narratifs", 61-62, Tzvetan Todorov, "Les Catégories du récit littéraire", 140, and Tzvetan Todorov, "Poétique", 137-138.

Alternation has been defined by Tzvetan Todorov as a way of presenting "deux histoires simultanément, en interrompant tantôt l'une tantôt l'autre, pour la reprendre à l'interruption suivante".[3] More specifically, in alternation, a narrative section of a component simple story A would be followed by a narrative section of a component simple story B, which in turn would be followed by a narrative section of A, and so on and so forth. Both (3) and (4) above provide examples of alternation, but note that (3) combines two simple stories, (9) and (10), which have one narrative event in common:

(13) *John lost a lot of money.*

As for embedding, it is a device by means of which an entire simple story is placed between the first and the second narrative section of another simple story. Both (5) and (6) above are examples of embedding. In (5), for instance,

(14) *Joan was poor, then Joan made money, then, as a result, she was rich*

is placed between the first and the second narrative section of

(15) *John was rich, then John lost money, then, as a result, he was poor.*

4.2 A complex story may be constituted by more than two simple stories. Consider, for example, the following:

(16) *On Monday, John was happy, then he met Joan, then, as a result, he was unhappy. Then on Tuesday, Peter was happy, then he met Joan, then, as a result, he was unhappy. Then, on Wednesday, James was happy, then he met Joan, then, as a result, he was unhappy*

(17) *John was unhappy and Peter was sick and James was poor. Then John met Mary and Peter took some medicine and James found a lot of money. Then, as a result, John was happy and Peter was healthy and James was rich*

[3] Tzvetan Todorov, "Les Catégories du récit littéraire", 140.

(18) *John was unhappy and Peter was sick and James was poor. Then James found a lot of money, then, as a result, he was rich. Then Peter took some medicine, then, as a result, he was healthy. Then John met Mary, then, as a result, he was happy.*

(16) is made up of three conjoined simple stories, (17) of three alternating simple stories, and (18) of one simple story embedded in another which in turn is embedded in another. A fourth simple story could, of course be conjoined with (16), or made to alternate with the three alternating stories in (17), or again be embedded in the most deeply embedded simple story of (18); and so on. Thus, there is no upper limit to the number of simple stories which may constitute a complex story.

4.2.1 The commonness of a given combinational pattern varies according to the medium through which complex stories are expressed. Alternation, for instance, is rarely used in oral narrative[4] but is quite popular in written narrative. Moreover, repeated multiple embedding is seldom found in stories expressed through oral language or moving pictures whereas it is a rather common feature of stories expressed through written language. These variations are at least partially due to the fact that an audience finds it almost impossible to follow an oral narrative or a movie in which multiple embedding and alternation abound but does not experience much difficulty in following a written narrative organized around the same patterns.

4.2.2 (2) and (3) above derive a certain amount of cohesion from the fact that a narrative event in one of the two component simple stories is also a narrative event in the other one. In general, the more narrative events component simple stories have in common, the more a complex story tends to be cohesive.[5]

[4] Tzvetan Todorov even writes in "Les Catégories du récit littéiaire", 140: "Cette forme [l'alternance] caractérise évidemment des genres littéraires ayant perdu toute liaison avec la littérature orale: celle-ci ne peut pas connaître l'alternance".
[5] Of course, two component simple stories may not have three narrative events in common.

Another common way of giving a complex story a certain degree of cohesion is to have the various simple stories constituting it share a feature in common, whether it be a protagonist, or a theme, or an action, or a combination of all three. In (1), for instance, each of the two component simple stories presents a character who becomes very rich; and in (2), both component simple stories have the same protagonist and both tell of his encounter with a woman and its results.

Note, however, that in a complex story component simple stories do not have to share a protagonist, or a theme, or what-not. Consider the following complex stories, each made up of two simple stories:

(19) *John was happy, then he met Joan, then, as a result, he was unhappy. Then, as a result, Peter was black, then he saw a bird, then, as a result, he was white*

(20) *John was happy and Peter was black, then John met Joan and Peter saw a bird, then, as a result, John was unhappy and Peter was white*

(21) *John was happy and Peter was black. Then Peter saw a bird, then, as a result, he was white. Then John met Joan, then, as a result, he was unhappy.*

(19), (20), and (21) have the same structure as (1), (4), and (5) respectively and are as grammatical (can be accounted for by the same rules of grammar). Nevertheless, it is clear that (19), (20), and (21) constitute less acceptable stories than (1), (4), and (5). Two stories may thus be equally grammatical but not equally acceptable, the acceptability of a given story depending not only on its grammaticality but also on other factors more difficult to define, such as context.[6]

4.3 Several combinational patterns may be found in the same complex story. Consider the following:

[6] Though all the stories I have used in the course of this study are grammatical, many of them may be less than acceptable to some readers.

(22) *John was rich and Joan was poor. Then Joan made a lot of money, then, as a result, she was rich. Then John lost a lot of money, then, as a result, he was poor. Then he made a lot of money, then, as a result, he was rich*

(23) *John was happy and Joan was unhappy, then John got divorced and Joan got married, then, as a result, John was unhappy and Joan was happy. Then Joan met Jack, then, as a result, she was unhappy*

(24) *John was happy and Joan was unhappy and Peter was poor. Then Peter found a lot of money, then, as a result, he was rich. Then John met Mary and Joan met James, then, as a result, John was unhappy and Joan was happy*

(25) *John was happy and Joan was unhappy and Peter was poor. Then Peter found a lot of money, then, as a result, he was rich. Then John met Mary and Joan met James, then, as a result, John was unhappy and Joan was happy. Then she met Jack, then, as a result, she was unhappy.*

In (22), one story is embedded in another and both are conjoined with a third one; in (23), one story is conjoined with two alternating stories; in (24), there is one example of embedding and one of alternation; and in (25), we find all three combinational patterns, embedding, alternation, and conjoining.

4.3.1 The kind of combinational pattern used in a complex story constitutes an important characteristic of that story. For example, it determines at least partially the rate at which various component simple stories unfold. If one story is embedded in another, the development of the latter is obviously delayed. It would be delayed even more if a third story were embedded in the originally embedded story, and so on and so forth. On the other hand, the evolvement of a component simple story is in no way altered when a story or group of stories is conjoined with it.

In general, the kind of combinational pattern favored in a complex story is related to the goals of the storyteller. In adventure novels, for instance, conjoining is very common. In simultaneist novels — *1919* or *Le Sursis* — alternation is relatively abundant. The same is true of epistolary novels such as *Les Liaisons dangereuses* and *La Nouvelle-Héloïse*. In a novel like *A la recherche du temps perdu*, where one story interrupts another one only to be itself interrupted by a third one, embedding plays an unusually important role. This is one of the reasons for which Proust's masterpiece is so very similar to several more recent novels: in works like *La Route des Flandres* or *The Floating Opera*, the development of a given component simple story is systematically abandoned for that of another one.

4.4   In order to account for the structure of stories like (1)-(6), it is necessary to add a new set of rules to the rules which we already have. Like the rules in 3.5, these rules will be transformational. However, whereas the former are singular transformations and operate on a single string, the new rules are generalized transformations and operate on two strings, provided these strings have a certain structure.[7] Generalized transformations can conjoin such strings, embed one into another, or have their substrings alternate.

The first part of a generalized transformation is a structural analysis specifying the kind of strings (in term of their structure) to which the rule applies. A rule might apply for instance to any two stories which can be analyzed as follows:

SA: of (a): N Sec – CCL – N Sec – CCL – N Sec
　　 of (b): N Sec – CCL – N Sec – CCL – N Sec

The second part of the rule specifies the structural change by means of numbers referring to the segments specified by the structural analysis. Given SA above, 1-5 would refer to the segments in (a), 6-10 to the segments in (b), and the structural change might be:

---

[7]   In my elaboration of generalized transformations, I follow Chomsky's *Syntactic Structures*, "On the Notion 'Rule of Grammar'", "A Transformational Approach to Syntax", and Emmon Bach, *An Introduction to Transformational Grammars*.

SC: $(1 - 2 - 3 - 4 - 5;\ 6 - 7 - 8 - 9 - 10) \rightarrow 1 - 2 - 3 - 4 - 5 -$ CCL $- 6 - 7 - 8 - 9 - 10$

Note that, like in singulary transformations, it is sometimes necessary to describe certain conditions that must be met in addition to those specified in the structural analysis.

4.5 Complex stories such as (1) could be accounted for if we applied the following generalized transformations:

GT_{1a}: SA: of (a): N Sec – CCL – N Sec – CCL – N Sec
of (b): St
SC: $(1 - 2 - 3 - 4 - 5;\ 6) \rightarrow 1 - 2 - 3 - 4 - 5 - $ CCL $- 6$

The rule indicates that any kernel simple story may be conjoined with another story by a cluster of conjunctive features.

(7) and (8) which are component simple stories in (1) may be represented by tree diagrams (26) and (27) respectively. Applying GT_{1a} to (26) and (27) would yield (1), which could be represented by diagram (28).

Various other generalized transformations would help us account for the structure of other complex stories. Thus,

GT_{1b}: SA: of (a): N Sec – CCL – N Sec – CCL – N Sec
of (b): N Sec – CCL – N Sec – CCL – N Sec
SC: $(1 - 2 - 3 - 4 - 5;\ 6 - 7 - 8 - 9 - 10) \rightarrow 1 - 2 - 3 - 4 -$ $5 - 7 - 8 - 9 - 10$
(where $5 = 6$)
GT_{2a}: SA: of (a): N Sec – CCL – N Sec – CCL – N Sec
of (b): N Sec – CCL – N Sec – CCL – N Sec
SC: $(1 - 2 - 3 - 4 - 5;\ 6 - 7 - 8 - 9 - 10) \rightarrow 1 - CF_{and} -$ $6 - 2 - 3 - 4 - 5 - CF_{and} - 10$
(where $2 = 7;\ 4 = 9;\ 3 = 8$)
GT_{2b}: SA: of (a): N Sec – CCL – N Sec – CCL – N Sec
of (b): N Sec – CCL – N Sec – CCL – N Sec

(26)

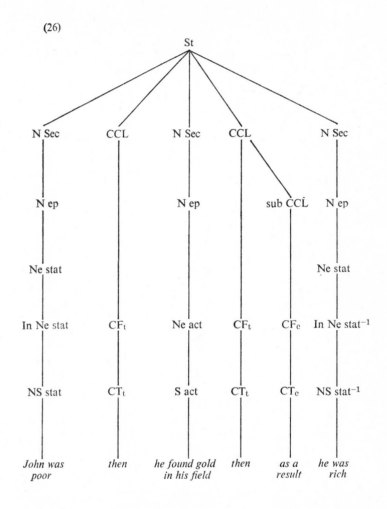

$$SC: (1 - 2 - 3 - 4 - 5; 6 - 7 - 8 - 9 - 10) \rightarrow 1 - CF_{and} -$$
$$6 - 2 - 3 - CF_{and} - 8 - 4 - 5 - CF_{and} - 10$$
$$(\text{where } 2 = 7; 4 = 9)$$

GT_3: SA: of (a): N Sec – CCL – N Sec – CCL – N Sec
of (b): St

$$SC: (1 - 2 - 3 - 4 - 5; 6) \rightarrow 1 - CF_{and} - 6 - 2 - 3 - 4 - 5$$

(27)

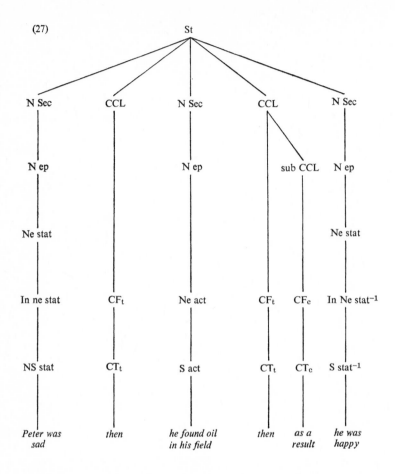

would help assign a structure to (2)-(6).[8]

So far, I have shown how the structure of some complex stories can be accounted for by applying a single transformational rule to two strings yielded by grammar G. There are complex stories the structure of which can be accounted for only through the use of more than one generalized transformation. Generalized trans-

[8]   Once again, I am giving GT_{1a}-GT_3 simply as possible examples of rules that would help account for the structure of complex stories.

(28)

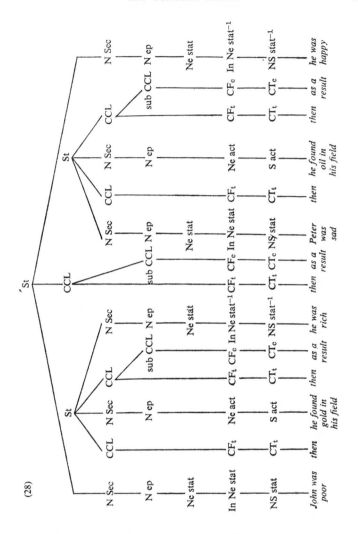

formations should therefore operate in such a way that they can apply not only to structures yielded by grammar G but also to structures that are the products of transformations. Of course, the new product itself should be capable of undergoing further changes. Consider, for instance:

(29) *John was poor, then he met Joan, then, as a result, he was rich.*
Then, as a result, Peter was poor, then he met Mary, then, as
a result, he was rich. Then, as a result, Jack was poor, then
he met Ethel, then, as a result, he was rich.

Applying GT₁ₐ to

(30) *Peter was poor, then he met Mary, then, as a result, he was*
rich

and

(31) *Jack was poor, then he met Ethel, then, as a result, he was rich*

would yield

(32) *Peter was poor, then he met Mary, then, as a result, he was*
rich. Then, as a result, Jack was poor, then he met Ethel, then,
as a result, he was rich.

Applying GT₁ₐ to

(33) *John was poor, then he met Joan, then, as a result, he was rich*

and (32) would yield (29), which could be represented by the
simplified diagram (34).

(34)

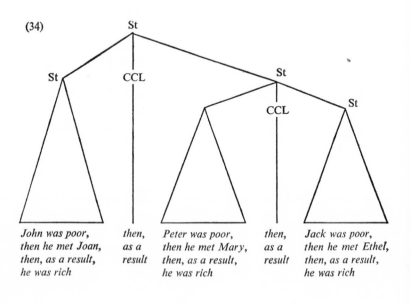

The structure of some complex stories can be accounted for not only through the application of generalized transformations but also through that of singulary transformations. Thus, the structure of

(35) *John was poor; before John was poor, John had been rich; after John was poor, John worked very hard; then, as a result, John was rich. Then John met Mary, then, as a result, John was poor*

would be accounted for by: a) applying GT_{1b} to

(36) *John had been rich, then John was poor, then John worked very hard, then, as a result, John was rich*

and

(37) *John was rich, then he met Mary, then, as a result, John was poor*

which would yield

(38) *John had been rich, then John was poor, then John worked very hard, then, as a result, John was rich, then he met Mary, then, as a result, John was poor;*

b) applying T_{1b} to (38).[9]

In conclusion, note that, given the appropriate generalized transformations, it would ideally be possible to account for the structure of any complex story.

---

[9]   Like singulary transformations, generalized transformations probably have to be (partially) ordered. At this point, however, it is clearly not possible to determine the order in which generalized transformations must apply. Nor is it possible to decide whether all generalized transformations should apply before singulary transformations or not.

APPENDIX

As a more concrete illustration of the possibilities of the system I have presented, I propose to describe the structure of Perrault's version of *Little Red Riding Hood* in terms of it. I am choosing this tale because it is very well-known and because it is short. Note that, in translating the tale from the French, I have tried to be as faithful to the original as possible. Note also that, for the sake of convenience and brevity, I will often assume that parts of the tale which are derived from two or more discrete elementary strings represent only one event.

A. *The Text*. — Once upon a time there was a little country girl, the prettiest little girl one could see; her mother was crazy about her and her grandmother even crazier. This good woman had had made for her a little red riding hood which became her so much that she was called Little Red Riding Hood everywhere.

One day, her mother having baked and made girdle-cakes said to her: "Go see how your grandmother is, for I was told that she was sick. Take her a girdle-cake and this little pot of butter." Little Red Riding Hood left immediately to go to her grandmother, who lived in another village. Passing through a wood, she met Brother Wolf who felt very much like eating her; but he did not dare because of some woodcutters who were in the forest. He asked her where she was going. The poor child, who did not know that it was dangerous to stop and listen to a wolf, told him: "I am going to see my grandmother and bring her a girdle-cake, with a little pot of butter that my mother is sending her". — "Does she

live very far?", said the Wolf to her. — "Oh! yes", said Little Red
Riding Hood, "it is beyond the mill that you see over there, by the
first house of the village." — "Well!", said the Wolf, "I want to go
see her too: I will go there this way, and you that way; and we
will see who gets there sooner."

The Wolf took the shortest way and started to run with all his
might, and the little girl went the longest way and had a good
time gathering hazel-nuts, running after butterflies, and making
bouquets out of the little flowers she saw.

The Wolf was not long in getting to the grandmother's house;
he knocks: tap, tap. — "Who is there?" — "It's your daughter,
Little Red Riding Hood", said the Wolf disguising his voice,
"bringing you a girdle-cake and a little pot of butter that my
mother sends you." The good grandmother, who was in her bed
because she was slightly ill, called out to him: "Pull the bolt, the
wooden-latch will fall". The Wolf pulled the bolt and the door
opened. He threw himself on the good woman and devoured her
in no time, for it had been more than three days since he had
eaten. Then he closed the door and went to lie down in the grandmother's bed, waiting for Little Red Riding Hood who, after a
time, came knocking at the door: tap, tap. — "Who is there?"
Little Red Riding Hood, who heard the Wolf's gruff voice, was
frightened at first but, thinking that her grandmother had a cold,
answered: "It's your daughter, Little Red Riding Hood, bringing
you a girdle-cake and a little pot of butter that my mother sends
you". The Wolf, softening his voice a little, called out to her:
"Pull the bolt, the wooden-latch will fall". Little Red Riding Hood
pulled the bolt and the door opened.

The Wolf, seeing her enter, told her as he hid in the bed, under
the cover: "Put the girdle-cake and the little pot of butter on the
bin and come lie down next to me". Little Red Riding Hood
undresses and gets into bed, where she was very surprised to see
what her grandmother looked like in her dishabille. She told her:
"Grandmother, you have such big arms!" — "It's to kiss you
better, my child!" — "Grandmother, you have such big legs!" —
"It's to run better, my child!" "Grandmother, you have such big

ears!" — "It's to listen better, my child!" — "Grandmother, you have such big eyes!" — "It's to see you better my child!" — "Grandmother, you have such big teeth!" — "It's to eat you!" And, as he said these words, this naughty Wolf threw himself on Little Red Riding Hood and ate her.

B. If we apply the rules of Grammar G, we get:
  (a) by applying rule 1,

St $\rightarrow$ N Sec + CCL + N Sec + CCL + N Sec

  (b) by applying rule 2,

Ep + CCL + Nep + CCL + Ep + CCL + Nep + CCL + Nep

  (c) by applying rules 3 and 4 alternately and after forty-five applications of rule 3 and forty-four applications of rule 4.

ep_1 + CCL + ep_2 + CCL + ep_3 + CCL + ep_4 + CCL + ep_5 + CCL + ep_6 + CCL + ep_7 + CCL + Nep_1 + CCL + ep_8 + CCL + ep_9 + CCL + ep_{10} + CCL + ep_{11} + CCL + ep_{12} + CCL + ep_{13} + CCL + ep_{14} + CCL + ep_{15} + CCL + ep_{16} + CCL + ep_{17} + CCL + ep_{18} + CCL + ep_{19} + CCL + ep_{20} + CCL + ep_{21} + CCL + ep_{22} + CCL + ep_{23} + CCL + ep_{24} + CCL + ep_{25} + CCL + ep_{26} + CCL + ep_{27} + CCL + ep_{28} + CCL + ep_{29} + CCL + ep_{30} + CCL + ep_{31} + CCL + ep_{32} + CCL + ep_{33} + CCL + ep_{34} + CCL + ep_{35} + CCL + ep_{36} + CCL + ep_{37} + CCL + ep_{38} + CCL + ep_{39} + CCL + ep_{40} + CCL + ep_{41} + CCL + ep_{42} + CCL + ep_{43} + CCL + ep_{44} + CCL + ep_{45} + CCL + ep_{46} + CCL + ep_{47} + CCL + ep_{48} + CCL + ep_{49} + CCL + ep_{50} + CCL + ep_{51} + CCL + ep_{52} + CCL + Nep_2 + CCL + Nep_3

  (d) by applying rule 5,

ep_1 + CF_t + ep_2 + CF_t + ep_3 + CF_t + ep_4 + CF_t + sub CCL + ep_5 + CF_t + ep_6 + CF_t + ep_7 + CF_t + Nep_1 + CF_t + ep_8 + CF_t + sub CCL + ep_9 + CF_t + ep_{10} + CF_t + ep_{11} + CF_t + ep_{12} + CF_t + ep_{13} + CF_t + ep_{14} + CF_t + ep_{15} + CF_t + ep_{16} + CF_t + ep_{17} + CF_t + ep_{18} + CF_t + ep_{19} + CF_t + sub CCL + ep_{20} + CF_t + ep_{21} + CF_t + sub CCL + ep_{22} +

CF_t + ep_{23} + CF_t + ep_{24} + CF_t + sub CCL + ep_{25} + CF_t + ep_{26} + CF_t + ep_{27} + CF_t + ep_{28} + CF_t + ep_{29} + CF_t + ep_{30} + CF_t + ep_{31} + CF_t + ep_{32} + CF_t + sub CCL + ep_{33} + CF_t + sub CCL + ep_{34} + CF_t + ep_{35} + CF_t + ep_{36} + CF_t + sub CCL + ep_{37} + CF_t + ep_{38} + CF_t + ep_{39} + CF_t + sub CCL + ep_{40} + CF_t + ep_{41} + CF_t + ep_{42} + CF_t + ep_{43} + CF_t + ep_{44} + CF_t + ep_{45} + CF_t + ep_{46} + CF_t + ep_{47} + CF_t + ep_{48} + CF_t + ep_{49} + CF_t + ep_{50} + CF_t + ep_{51} + CF_t + ep_{52} + CF_t + Nep_2 + CF_t + sub CCL + Nep_3

(e) by applying rule 6, the same as (d) except that

$Nep_1 \longrightarrow$ E stat + sub CCL + Ne $stat_1$

$Nep_2 \longrightarrow$ Ne act

$Nep_3 \longrightarrow$ Ne $stat_2$

(f) by applying rule 7,

E $stat_1$ + CF_t + E $stat_2$ + CF_t + E act_1 + CF_t + E act_2 + CF_t + sub CCL + E act_3 + CF_t + E act_4 + CF_t + E act_5 + CF_t + E $stat_3$ + sub CCL + Ne $stat_1$ + CF_t + E act_6 + CF_t + sub CCL + E act_7 + CF_t + E act_8 + CF_t + E act_t + CF_t + E act_{10} + CF_t + E act_{11} + CF_t + E act_{12} + CF_t + E $stat_4$ + CF_t + E act_{13} + CF_t + E act_{14} + CF_t + E act_{15} + CF_t + E act_{16} + CF_t + sub CCL + E act_{17} + CF_t + E act_{18} + CF_t + sub CCL + E act_{19} + CF_t + E act_{20} + CF_t + E $stat_5$ + CF_t + sub CCL + E act_{21} + CF_t + E act_{22} + CF_t + E act_{23} + CF_t + E act_{24} + CF_t + E act_{25} + CF_t + E act_{26} + CF_t + E act_{27} + CF_t + E $stat_6$ + CF_t + sub CCL + E act_{28} + CF_t + sub CCL + E act_{29} + CF_t + E act_{30} + CF_t + E act_{31} + CF_t + sub CCL + E act_{32} + CF_t + E act_{33} + CF_t + E act_{34} + CF_t + sub CCL + E act_{35} + CF_t + E act_{36} + CF_t + E $stat_7$ + CF_t + E act_{37} + CF_t + E act_{38} + CF_t + E act_{39} + CF_t + E act_{40} + CF_t + E act_{41} + CF_t + E act_{42} + CF_t + E act_{43} + CF_t + E act_{44} + CF_t + E act_{45} + CF_t + E act_{46} + CF_t + Ne act + CF_t + sub CCL + Ne $stat_2$

(g) by applying rules 8 and 9 alternately and after nine applications of rule 8 and eight applications of rule 9, e stat$_1$ + sub CCL + e stat$_2$ + sub CCL + e stat$_3$ + sub CCL + e stat$_4$ + sub CCL + e stat$_5$ + sub CCL + e stat$_6$ + sub CCL + e stat$_7$ + sub CCL + e stat$_8$ + sub CCL + e stat$_9$ + CF$_t$ + e stat$_{10}$ + sub CCL + e stat$_{11}$ + sub CCL + e stat$_{12}$ + CF$_t$ + E act$_1$ + CF$_t$ + E act$_2$ + CF$_t$ + sub CCL + E act$_3$ + CF$_t$ + E act$_4$ + CF$_t$ + E act$_5$ + CF$_t$ + e stat$_{13}$ + sub CCL + Ne stat$_1$ + CF$_t$ + E act$_6$ + CF$_t$ + sub CCL + E act$_7$ + CF$_t$ + E act$_8$ + CF$_t$ + E act$_9$ + CF$_t$ + E act$_{10}$ + CF$_t$ + E act$_{11}$ + CF$_t$ + E act$_{12}$ + CF$_t$ + e stat$_{14}$ + sub CCL + e stat$_{15}$ + sub CCL + e stat$_{16}$ + sub CCL + e stat$_{17}$ + CF$_t$ + E act$_{13}$ + CF$_t$ + E act$_{14}$ + CF$_t$ + E act$_{15}$ + CF$_t$ + E act$_{16}$ + CF$_t$ + sub CCL + E act$_{17}$ + CF$_t$ + E act$_{18}$ + CF$_t$ + sub CCL + E act$_{19}$ + CF$_t$ + E act$_{20}$ + CF$_t$ + e stat$_{18}$ + CF$_t$ + sub CCL + E act$_{21}$ + CF$_t$ + E act$_{22}$ + CF$_t$ + E act$_{23}$ + CF$_t$ + E act $_{24}$ + CF$_t$ + E act$_{25}$ + CF$_t$ + E act$_{26}$ + CF$_t$ + E act$_{27}$ + CF$_t$ + e stat$_{19}$ + CF$_t$ + sub CCL + E act$_{28}$ + CF$_t$ + sub CCL + E act$_{29}$ + CF$_t$ + E act$_{30}$ + CF$_t$ + E act$_{31}$ + CF$_t$ + sub CCL + E act$_{32}$ + CF$_t$ + E act$_{33}$ + CF$_t$ + E act$_{34}$ + sub CCL + CF$_t$ + E act$_{35}$ + CF$_t$ + E act$_{36}$ + CF$_t$ + e stat$_{20}$ + CF$_t$ + E act$_{37}$ + CF$_t$ + E act$_{38}$ + CF$_t$ + E act$_{39}$ + CF$_t$ + E act$_{40}$ + CF$_t$ + E act$_{41}$ + CF$_t$ + E act$_{42}$ + CF$_t$ + E act$_{43}$ + CF$_t$ + E act$_{44}$ + CF$_t$ + E act$_{45}$ + CF$_t$ + E act$_{46}$ + CF$_t$ + Ne act + CF$_t$ + sub CCL + Ne stat$_2$

(h) by applying rules 10 and 11 alternately and after two applications of rule 10 and one application of rule 11,

e stat$_1$ + sub CCL + e stat$_2$ + sub CCL + e stat$_3$ + sub CCL + e stat$_4$ + sub CCL + e stat$_5$ + sub CCL + e stat$_6$ + sub CCL + e stat$_7$ + sub CCL + e stat$_8$ + sub CCL + e stat$_9$ + CF$_t$ + e stat$_{10}$ + sub CCL + e stat$_{11}$ + sub CCL + e stat$_{12}$ + CF$_t$ + e act$_1$ + sub CCL + e act$_2$ + CF$_t$ + e act$_3$ + CF$_t$ + sub CCL + e act$_4$ + CF$_t$ + e act$_5$ + CF$_t$ + e act$_6$ + CF$_t$ + e stat$_{13}$ + sub CCL + Ne stat$_1$ + CF$_t$ + e act$_7$ + CF$_t$ + sub CCL + e act$_8$ + CF$_t$ + e act$_9$ + CF$_t$ + e act$_{10}$ + CF$_t$ + e act$_{11}$ + CF$_t$ + e act$_{12}$ + CF$_t$ + e act$_{13}$ + CF$_t$ + e stat$_{14}$ + sub CCL + e stat$_{15}$ + sub CCL + e stat$_{16}$ + sub CCL + e stat$_{17}$ + CF$_t$

+ e act$_{14}$ + CF$_t$ + e act$_{15}$ + CF$_t$ + e act$_{16}$ + CF$_t$ + e act$_{17}$ + sub CCL + e act$_{18}$ + CF$_t$ + sub CCL + e act$_{19}$ + CF$_t$ + e act$_{20}$ + CF$_t$ + sub CCL + e act$_{21}$ + CF$_t$ + e act$_{22}$ + CF$_t$ + e stat$_{18}$ + CF$_t$ + sub CCL + e act$_{23}$ + CF$_t$ + e act$_{24}$ + CF$_t$ + e act$_{25}$ + CF$_t$ + e act$_{26}$ + CF$_t$ + e act$_{27}$ + CF$_t$ + e act$_{28}$ + CF$_t$ + e act$_{29}$ + CF$_t$ + e stat$_{19}$ + CF$_t$ + sub CCL + e act$_{30}$ + CF$_t$ + sub CCL + e act$_{31}$ + CF$_t$ + e act$_{32}$ + sub CCL + e act$_{33}$ + CF$_t$ + e act$_{34}$ + CF$_t$ + sub CCL + e act$_{35}$ + CF$_t$ + e act$_{36}$ + CF$_t$ + e act$_{37}$ + sub CCL + e act$_{38}$ + CF$_t$ + sub CCL + e act$_{39}$ + CF$_t$ + e act$_{40}$ + CF$_t$ + e stat$_{20}$ + CF$_t$ + e act$_{41}$ + CF$_t$ + e act$_{42}$ + CF$_t$ + e act$_{43}$ + CF$_t$ + e act$_{44}$ + CF$_t$ + e act$_{45}$ + CF$_t$ + e act$_{46}$ + CF$_t$ + e act$_{47}$ + CF$_t$ + e act$_{48}$ + CF$_t$ + e act$_{49}$ + CF$_t$ + e act$_{50}$ + sub CCL + e act$_{51}$ + CF$_t$ + Ne act + CF$_t$ + sub CCL + Ne stat$_2$

(i) by applying 12, the same as (h) except that

Ne stat$_1$ $\longrightarrow$ In Ne stat
Ne stat$_2$ $\longrightarrow$ In Ne stat^{-1}

(j) by applying 13,

e stat$_1$ + CF$_n$ + e stat$_2$ + CF$_n$ + e stat$_3$ + CF$_n$ + e stat$_4$ + CF$_n$ + e stat$_5$ + CF$_n$ + e stat$_6$ + CF$_c$ + e stat$_7$ + CF$_n$ + e stat$_8$ + CF$_n$ + e stat$_9$ + CF$_t$ + e stat$_{10}$ + CF$_n$ + e stat$_{11}$ + CF$_n$ + e stat$_{12}$ + CF$_t$ + e act$_1$ + CF$_n$ + e act$_2$ + CF$_t$ + e act$_3$ + CF$_t$ + CF$_c$ + e act$_4$ + CF$_t$ + e act$_5$ + CF$_t$ + e act$_6$ + CF$_t$ + e stat$_{13}$ + CF$_c$ + In Ne stat + CF$_t$ + e act$_7$ + CF$_t$ + CF$_c$ + e act$_8$ + CF$_t$ + e act$_9$ + CF$_t$ + e act$_{10}$ + CF$_t$ + e act$_{11}$ + CF$_t$ + e act$_{12}$ + CF$_t$ + e act$_{13}$ + CF$_t$ + e stat$_{14}$ + CF$_n$ + e stat$_{15}$ + CF$_n$ + e stat$_{16}$ + CF$_n$ + e stat$_{17}$ + CF$_t$ + e act$_{14}$ + CF$_t$ + e act$_{15}$ + CF$_t$ + e act$_{16}$ + CF$_t$ + e act$_{17}$ + CF$_n$ + e act$_{18}$ + CF$_t$ + CF$_c$ + e act$_{19}$ + CF$_t$ + e act$_{20}$ + CF$_t$ + CF$_c$ + e act$_{21}$ + CF$_t$ + e act$_{22}$ + CF$_t$ + e stat$_{18}$ + CF$_t$ + CF$_c$ + e act$_{23}$ + CF$_t$ + e act$_{24}$ + CF$_t$ + e act$_{25}$ + CF$_t$ + e act$_{26}$ + CF$_t$ + e act$_{27}$ + CF$_t$ + e act$_{28}$ + CF$_t$ + e act$_{29}$ + CF$_t$ + e stat$_{19}$ + CF$_t$ + CF$_n$ + e act$_{30}$ + CF$_t$ + CF$_c$ + e act$_{31}$ + CF$_t$ + e act$_{32}$ + CF$_n$ + e act$_{33}$ + CF$_t$ + e act$_{34}$ + CF$_t$ + CF$_c$ + e act$_{35}$

$+ CF_t + e \ act_{36} + CF_t + e \ act_{37} + CF_n + e \ act_{38} + CF_t +$
$CF_c + e \ act_{39} + CF_t + e \ act_{40} + CF_t + e \ stat_{20} + CF_t + e \ act_{41}$
$+ CF_t + e \ act_{42} + CF_t + e \ act_{43} + CF_t + e \ act_{44} + CF_t +$
$e \ act_{45} + CF_t + e \ act_{46} + CF_t + e \ act_{47} + CF_t + e \ act_{48} +$
$CF_t + e \ act_{49} + CF_t + e \ act_{50} + CF_n + e \ act_{51} + CF_t + Ne \ act$
$+ CF_t + CF_c + In \ Ne \ stat^{-1}$

(k) by applying the appropriate expression rules, we get the following kernel simple story (conjunctive terms and sentences representing narrative events are underlined; the symbols at the left of each line identify each event as stative or active and specify its position in the story: thus $e \ stat_1$ would refer to the first stative event, $e \ act_1$ to the first active event, and so on; the various episodes and narrative episodes are separated by a symbol identifying them):

ep_1

Once upon a time there was a little country girl	$e \ stat_1$
and one could not see a prettier girl	$e \ stat_2$
and her mother was crazy about her	$e \ stat_3$
and her grandmother was even crazier about her	$e \ stat_4$
and her grandmother had had made for her a little red riding hood	$e \ stat_5$
and this little red riding hood became her very much	$e \ stat_6$
therefore she was called Little Red Riding Hood everywhere	$e \ stat_7$
and the grandmother lived in another village	$e \ stat_8$
and Little Red Riding Hood did not know that it was dangerous to stop and listen to a wolf	$e \ stat_9$

ep_2

then Brother Wolf had not eaten for more than three days	$e \ stat_{10}$
and the grandmother was in her bed	$e \ stat_{11}$
because she was slightly ill	$e \ stat_{12}$

ep_3
then, one day, the mother baked   e act_1
and she made girdle-cakes   e act_2

ep_4
then she said to Little Red Riding Hood to go see...
pot of butter   e act_3

ep_5
then, as a result, Little Red Riding Hood left immediately to go to her grandmother   e act_4

ep_6
then she passed through a wood   e act_5

ep_7
then she met Brother Wolf there   e act_6

N ep_1
then Brother Wolf felt very much like eating her   e $stat_{13}$
therefore a want was created in him   Ne $stat_1$

ep_8
then he thought of the woodcutters in the forest   e act_7

ep_9
then, as a result, he did not dare to eat her   e act_8

ep_{10}
then he asked her where she was going   e act_9

ep_{11}
then the poor child told him that she was going...
sending her   e act_{10}

ep_{12}
then the Wolf asked her whether her grandmother
lived very far   e act_{11}

ep$_{13}$

then Little Red Riding Hood answered that yes... of
the village   e act$_{12}$

ep$_{14}$

then the Wolf said that well... got there sooner   e act$_{13}$

ep$_{15}$

then the Wolf took the shortest way   e stat$_{14}$
and he started to run with all his might   e stat$_{15}$
and the little girl went the longest way   e stat$_{16}$
and she had a good time gathering hazel-nuts... she
saw   e stat$_{17}$

ep$_{16}$

then the Wolf was not long in getting to the grandmother's house   e act$_{14}$

ep$_{17}$

then he knocked tap, tap   e act$_{15}$

ep$_{18}$

then the grandmother asked who was there   e act$_{16}$

ep$_{19}$

then the Wolf disguised his voice   e act$_{17}$
and he said that it was her daughter... sent her   e act$_{18}$

ep$_{20}$

then, as a result, the good grandmother called out to
him to pull... would fall   e act$_{19}$

ep$_{21}$

then the Wolf pulled the bolt   e act$_{20}$

ep$_{22}$

then, as a result, the door opened   e act$_{21}$

ep$_{23}$
then he threw himself on the good woman   e act$_{22}$

ep$_{24}$
then he still had not eaten for more than three days   e stat$_{18}$

ep$_{25}$
then, as a result, he devoured her in no time   e act$_{23}$

ep$_{26}$
then he closed the door   e act$_{24}$

ep$_{27}$
then he went to lie down in the grandmother's bed   e act$_{25}$

ep$_{28}$
then he waited for Little Red Riding Hood   e act$_{26}$

ep$_{29}$
then, after a time, Little Red Riding Hood came
knocking at the door tap, tap   e act$_{27}$

ep$_{30}$
then the Wolf asked who was there   e act$_{28}$

ep$_{31}$
then Little Red Riding Hood heard the Wolf's gruff
voice   e act$_{29}$

ep$_{32}$
then, at first, she was frightened   e stat$_{19}$

ep$_{33}$
then, however, she thought that her grandmother had
a cold   e act$_{30}$

ep$_{34}$
then, as a result, she answered that it was... sent her   e act$_{31}$

ep_{35}

then the Wolf softened his voice   e act_{32}

and he called out to her to pull... would fall   e act_{33}

ep_{36}

then Little Red Riding Hood pulled the bolt   e act_{34}

ep_{37}

then, *as a result*, the door opened   e act_{35}

ep_{38}

then, the Wolf saw her enter   e act_{36}

ep_{39}

then he hid in the bed, under the cover   e act_{37}

and he told her to put the girdle-cake... next to him   e act_{38}

ep_{40}

then, *as a result*, Little Red Riding Hood undressed   e act_{39}

ep_{41}

then she got into the bed   e act_{40}

ep_{42}

then she was very surprised to see what her grand-
mother looked like in her dishabille   e $stat_{20}$

ep_{43}

then she told her grandmother that she had very big
arms   e act_{41}

ep_{44}

then the grandmother answered her child that it was
to kiss her better   e act_{42}

ep_{45}

then she told her grandmother that she had very big
legs   e act_{43}

ep$_{46}$

then the grandmother answered her child that it was
to run better   e act$_{44}$

ep$_{47}$

then she told her grandmother that she had very big
ears   e act$_{45}$

ep$_{48}$

then the grandmother answered her child that it was
to listen better   e act$_{46}$

ep$_{49}$

then she told her grandmother that she had very big
eyes   e act$_{47}$

ep$_{50}$

then the grandmother answered her child that it was
to see better   e act$_{48}$

ep$_{51}$

then she told her grandmother that she had very big
teeth   e act$_{49}$

ep$_{52}$

then the grandmother answered that it was to eat her   e act$_{50}$
and this naughty Wolf threw himself on Little Red
Riding Hood   e act$_{51}$

N ep$_2$
then he ate her   Ne act

N ep$_3$
then, as a result, a want was eliminated in him   Ne stat$_2$

C. Given the above kernel simple story,
   (a) by applying T$_{1c}$, we get

SA: X – Str ev – CF_n – e $stat_9$ – CF_t – Str ep – CCL – ep_{11} – CF_t – Str ep – Y

SC: $1 - 2 - 3 - 4 - 5 - 6 - 7 - 8 - 9 - 10 - 11 \rightarrow 1 - 2 - 5 - 6 - 7 - 8 - 3 -$ before 5 at the same time as $2 - 4 - 9 - 10 - 11$

which would be represented by:
Once upon a time there was a little country girl ... and the grand-mother lived in another village; then Brother Wolf had not eaten in more than three days ... then he asked her where she was going, then the poor child told him that she was going and (before: then Brother Wolf ... at the same time as: once upon a time ...). Little Red Riding Hood did not know that it was dangerous to stop and listen to a wolf; then the Wolf asked her whether her grandmother...

  (b) by applying T_{1c} again, we get

SA: X – Str ev – CF_n – e $stat_8$ – CF_t – Str ep – CCL – ep_5 – CF_t – Str ep – Y

SC: $1 - 2 - 3 - 4 - 5 - 6 - 7 - 8 - 9 - 10 - 11 \rightarrow 1 - 2 - 5 - 6 - 7 - 8 - 3 -$ before 5 at the same time as $2 - 4 - 9 - 10 - 11$

which would be represented by:
Once upon a time there was a little country girl ... therefore she was called Little Red Riding Hood everywhere; then Brother Wolf had not eaten in more than three days ... then she said to Little Red Riding Hood ... then, as a result Little Red Riding Hood left immediately to go to her grandmother and (before: then Brother Wolf ... at the same time as: once upon a time ...) the grandmother lived in another village; then she passed through a wood...

  (c) by applying T_{1c} again, we get

SA: X – Str ev – CF_n – Str ev (e $stat_{11}$ CF_n e $stat_{12}$) – CF_t – Str ep – CCL – ep_{20} – CF_t – Str ep – Y

SC: $1 - 2 - 3 - 4 - 5 - 6 - 7 - 8 - 9 - 10 - 11 \rightarrow 1 - 2 - 5 - 6 - 7 - 8 - 3 -$ before 5 at the same time as $2 - 4 - 9 - 10 - 11$

which would be represented by:
Brother Wolf had not eaten in more than three days ... then, one day, the mother baked ... then, as a result, the grandmother called out to him ... and (before: then, one day, the mother baked, at the same time as: Brother Wolf ...) the grandmother was in her bed because she was slightly ill; then the Wolf pulled the bolt...

(d) by applying T_{2b}, we get

SA: $X - Str\ ep - CF_t - ep_8 - CF_t - CF_c - ep_9 - CF_t - Str\ ep - Y$
SC: $1 - 2 - 3 - 4 - 5 - 6 - 7 - 8 - 9 - 10 \rightarrow 1 - 2 - 3 - 7 - CF$
   because $-$ before 7 after $2 - 4 - 8 - 9 - 10$

which would be represented by:
Brother Wolf felt very much like eating her ... then he did not dare to eat her because (before: he did not dare ... after: he felt very much like eating her) he thought of the woodcutters in the forest; then he asked her where she was going...

(e) by applying T_{2b} again, we get

SA: $X - Str\ ep - CF_t - ep_{24} - CF_t - CF_c - ep_{25} - CF_t - Str\ ep - Y$
SC: $1 - 2 - 3 - 4 - 5 - 6 - 7 - 8 - 9 - 10 \rightarrow 1 - 2 - 3 - 7 - CF$
   because $-$ before 7 after $2 - 4 - 8 - 9 - 10$

which would be represented by:
he threw himself on the good woman, then he devoured her in no time because (before: he devoured her in no time, after: he threw himself on the good woman) he still had not eaten for more than three days; then he closed the door...

(f) by applying T_{3b}, we get

SA: $X - CCL - e\ stat_{10} - Y$
SC: $1 - 2 - 3 - 4 \rightarrow 1 - CCL - e\ stat_{10_0} - Y$

that is: / then Brother Wolf had not eaten for more than three days / is zeroed.

(g) by applying T_{3c}, we get

SA: $X - \text{sub CCL} - \text{Ne stat}_1 - Y$

SC: $1 - 2 - 3 - 4 \rightarrow 1 - \text{sub CCL}_0 - \text{Ne stat}_{10} - Y$

that is: / therefore a want was created in him / is zeroed.

(h) by applying T_{3a}, we get

SA: $X - \text{CCL} - \text{Ne stat}_2 - Y$

SC: $1 - 2 - 3 - 4 \rightarrow 1 - \text{CCL}_0 - \text{Ne stat}_{2_0} - Y$

that is: / then, as a result, a want was eliminated in him / is zeroed.

We now have the following simple story:

Once upon a time there was a little country girl and one could not see a prettier girl and her mother was crazy about her and her grandmother was even crazier about her and her grandmother had had made for her a little red riding hood and this little red riding hood became her very much therefore she was called Little Red Riding Hood everywhere.

Then, one day, the mother baked and she made girdle-cakes; then she said to Little Red Riding Hood to go see how her grand-mother was, for she had been told that she was sick, and to take her a girdle-cake and a little pot of butter. Then, as a result, Little Red Riding Hood left immediately to go to her grandmother and the grandmother lived in another village. Then she passed through a wood; then she met Brother Wolf there; then Brother Wolf felt very much like eating her; then he did not dare to eat her because he thought of the woodcutters in the forest; then he asked her where she was going; then the poor child told him that she was going to see her grandmother and bring her a girdle-cake, with a little pot of butter that her mother was sending her, and Little Red Riding Hood did not know that it was dangerous to stop and listen to a wolf. Then the Wolf asked her whether her grandmother lived very far; then Little Red Riding Hood answered that yes, that it was beyond the mill that he saw over there, by the first house of the village. Then the Wolf said that, well, he wanted to go see her too, that he would go there this way, and she that way, and that they would see who got there sooner.

Then the Wolf took the shortest way and he started to run with all his might; and the little girl went the longest way and she had a good time gathering hazel-nuts, running after butterflies, and making bouquets out of the little flowers she saw.

Then the Wolf was not long in getting to the grandmother's house; then he knocked, tap, tap; then the grandmother asked who was there; then the Wolf disguised his voice and he said that it was her daughter, Little Red Riding Hood, bringing her a girdle cake and a little pot of butter that her mother sent her; then, as a result, the good grandmother called out to him to pull the bolt so that the wooden latch would fall, and the grandmother was in her bed because she was slightly ill. Then the Wolf pulled the bolt; then, as a result, the door opened; then he threw himself on the good woman; then he devoured her in no time because he still had not eaten for more than three days. Then he closed the door; then he went to lie down in the grandmother's bed; then he waited for Little Red Riding Hood. Then, after a time, Little Red Riding Hood came knocking at the door tap, tap; then the Wolf asked who was there; then Little Red Riding Hood heard the Wolf's gruff voice; then, at first, she was frightened; then, however, she thought that her grandmother had a cold; then, as a result, she answered that it was her daughter, Little Red Riding Hood, bringing her a girdle-cake and a little pot of butter that her mother sent her; then the Wolf softened his voice and he called out to her to pull the bolt so that the wooden-latch would fall; then Little Red Riding Hood pulled the bolt; then, as a result, the door opened.

Then the Wolf saw her enter; then he hid in the bed, under the cover, and, at the same time he told her to put the girdle-cake and the little pot of butter on the bin and to come lie down next to him. Then, as a result, Little Red Riding Hood undressed; then she got into the bed; then she was very surprised to see what her grandmother looked like in her dishabille; then she told her grandmother that she had very big arms; then the grandmother answered her child that it was to kiss her better; then she told her grandmother that she had very big legs; then the grandmother answered her child that it was to run better; then she told her grandmother that she had very big ears; then the grandmother answered her child that it was to listen better; then she told her grandmother that she had very big eyes; then her grandmother answered her child that it was to see better; then she told her grandmother that she had very big teeth; then the grandmother answered that it was to eat her and, at the same time this naughty Wolf threw himself on Little Red Riding Hood, then he ate her.

The above simple story, described by grammar G and several singulary transformations, differs from Perrault's version of *Little Red Riding Hood* in style only. In structure and information content, it is identical with it.

CONCLUSION

The grammar of stories developed in this study consists of two main sets of rules: 1) a finite set of simple rewrite rules assigning a structure to any kernel simple story, that is, to any story which can be defined as follows: a) it contains one minimal story and only one (three narrative events and only three), b) its events are in spatio-chronological order, c) any event occurring at the same time as the second narrative event must appear before it, d) any event occurring at the same time as the last narrative event must appear after it; and 2) a finite set of transformational rules, including both singulary and generalized transformations; these operate on strings yielded by the first set of rules or strings that have already been transformed and account for the structure of stories that are not kernel simple stories, such as stories the events of which are not in spatio-chronological order, stories containing more than one minimal story, and so on.

As it stands, this grammar is capable of assigning a specific structure to all the sets and only the sets which are generally and intuitively recognized as stories and it allows for the determination of the exact relationship between the structures of any two such sets.

As it stands, this grammar is not without defects and it would have to undergo many more or less important changes in order to be completely satisfactory. It is to be hoped that such a more thoroughly worked out grammar would not only assign more precise structures to stories but also lead to a better understanding of the nature of stories and open up fruitful areas of investigation.

BIBLIOGRAPHY

Arrivé, Michel
1968 "Stylistique littéraire et sémiotique littéraire", *La Nouvelle Critique*, no. spécial, 171-174.
1969 "Postulats pour la description linguistique des textes littéraires", *Langue Française*, no. 3, 3-13.
Bach, Emmon
1964 *An Introduction to Transformational Grammars* (New York).
Balzac, Honoré de
1963 *Une Ténébreuse Affaire* (Paris, Le Livre de Poche).
Barthes, Roland
1966 "Introduction à l'analyse structurale des récits", *Communications*, no. 8, 1-27.
1968 "L'Effet de réel", *Communications*, no. 11, 84-88.
Bremond, Claude
1964 "Le Message narratif", *Communications*, no. 4, 4-32.
1966 "La Logique des possibles narratifs", *Communications*, no. 8, 60-76.
1968 "Postérité américaine de Propp", *Communications*, no. 11, 148-164.
Champigny, Robert
1963 *Le Genre romanesque* (Monte-Carlo).
Chomsky, Noam
1957 *Syntactic Structures* (The Hague).
1961a "On the Notion 'Rule of Grammar'", *Proceedings of the Twelfth Symposium in Applied Mathematics*, XII, 6-24.
1961b "Some Methodological Remarks on Generative Grammar", *Word*, XVII, 219-239.
1962 "A Transformational Approach to Syntax", in A. A. Hill, ed., *Proceedings of the 1958 Conference on Problems of Linguistic Analysis in English* (Austin, Texas), 124-158.
1965 *Aspects of the Theory of Syntax* (Cambridge, Mass.).
Deighton, Len
1966 *Billion Dollar Brain* (Middlesex, Penguin Books).
Dorfman, Eugene
1956 "The Structure of the Narrative: A Linguistic Approach", *History of Ideas Newsletter*, II, 63-67.

1969 *The Narreme in the Medieval Romance Epic: An Introduction to Narrative Structures* (Toronto).

Ducasse, C. J.

1968 *Truth, Knowledge and Causation* (London).

Dundes, Alan

1962a "Trends in Content Analysis: A Review Article", *Midwest Folklore*, XII, no. 1, 31-38.

1962b "From Etic to Emic Units in the Structural Study of Folktales", *Journal of American Folklore*, LXXV, 95-105.

1964 *The Morphology of North American Indian Folktales* (Helsinki).

Erlich, Victor

1955 *Russian Formalism: History-Doctrine* (The Hague).

Genette, Gérard

1968 "Vraisemblable et motivation", *Communications*, no. 11, 5-21.

Greimas, A. J.

1966a *Sémantique structurale; recherche de méthode* (Paris).

1966b "Eléments pour une théorie de l'interprétation du récit mythique", *Communications*, no. 8, 28-59.

1967 "La Structure des actants du récit, Essai d'approche générative", *Word*, XXIII, no. 1-2-3, 221-238.

Guenoun, Denis

1968 "A propos de l'analyse structurale des récits", *La Nouvelle Critique*, no. spécial, 65-70.

Harris, Zellig

1962 *String Analysis of Sentence Structure* (The Hague).

Hendricks, William O.

1965 "Linguistics and the Structural Analysis of Literary Texts", University of Illinois dissertation.

1967 "On the Notion 'Beyond the Sentence'", *Linguistics*, no. 37, 12-51.

Köngäs, Elli K. and Pierre Maranda

1962 "Structural Models in Folklore", *Midwest Folklore*, XII, no. 3, 133-192.

Kristeva, Julia

1968 "Problèmes de la structuration du texte", *La Nouvelle Critique*, no. spécial, 55-64.

1969 "Narration et transformation", *Semiotica*, I, no. 4, 422-448.

Labov, William and Joshua Waletzky

1966 "Narrative Analysis. Oral Versions of Personal Experience", *Essays on the Verbal and Visual Arts. Proceedings of the Annual Spring Meeting of the American Ethnological Society*, 12-44.

Lévi-Strauss, Claude

1958 *Anthropologie structurale* (Paris).

Mendilow, A. A.

1952 *Time and the Novel* (London).

Morin, Violette

1966 "L'Histoire drôle", *Communications*, no. 8, 102-119.

Neumayer, Peter F.
1969 "The Child as Storyteller: Teaching Literary Concepts Through Tacit Knowledge", *College English*, XXX, no. 7, 515-517.
Peytard, Jean
1968 "Rapports et interférences de la linguistique et de la littérature (introduction à une bibliographie)", *La Nouvelle Critique*, no. spécial, 8-16.
Pike, Kenneth L.
1964 "Discourse Analysis and Tagmeme Matrices", *Oceanic Linguistics*, III, no. 1, 5-25.
1967 *Language in Relation to a Unified Theory of the Structure of Human Behavior* (The Hague).
Postal, Paul
1964 *Constituent Structure. A Study of Contemporary Models of Syntactic Description* (The Hague).
Pouillon, Jean
1946 *Temps et roman* (Paris).
Piince, Ellen F.
1970 "*Be-ing*: A Synchronic and Diachronic Study", *Transformations and Discourse Analysis Papers*, no. 81, University of Pennsylvania.
Prince, Gerald
1968 *Métaphysique et technique dans l'œuvre romanesque de Sartre* (Genève).
1969 "Towards a Normative Criticism of the Novel", *Genre*, II, no. 1, 1-8.
1971 "On Readers and Listeners in Narrative", *Neophilologus*, LV, no. 2, 117-122.
Propp, Vladimir
1958 *Morphology of the Folktale* (Bloomington).
Scott, Charles T.
1969 "On Defining the Riddle: The Problem of a Structural Unit", *Genre*, II, no. 2, 129-142.
Todorov, Hristo
1968 "Logique et temps narratif", *Information sur les Sciences Sociales*, VII, no. 6, 41-49.
Todorov, Tzvetan
1965 *Théorie de la littérature* (Paris).
1966 "Les Catégories du récit littéraire", *Communications*, no. 8, 125-151.
1967 *Littérature et signification* (Paris).
1968a "Poétique", in Oswald Ducrot et al., *Qu'est-ce que le structuralisme?* (Paris), pp. 97-166.
1968b "La Grammaire du récit", *Langages*, no. 12, 94-102.
1969 "La Quête du récit", *Critique*, XXV, no. 262, 195-214.
1970 *Grammaire du Décameran* (The Hague).

INDEX

Active event, 29, 30, 31, 32, 41, 43, 47
Active sentence, 30, 32
Alternation, 72, 73, 74, 76
Aristotle, 48
Arrivé, Michel, 11

Bach, Emmon, 10, 32, 63, 77
Balzac, 43, 49, 62, 63
Barth, John, 58
Barthes, Roland, 9, 11, 12, 16, 17, 26, 63
Beckett, Samuel, 24
Boccacio, 17, 28
Bremond, Claude, 11, 12, 16, 20, 23, 72

Camus, Albert, 25
Causal relationship, 24, 25, 45
Causality, 25
Champigny, Robert, 23
Chomsky, Noam, 5, 10, 17, 32, 63, 77
Christie, Agatha, 43
Chronological order, 22, 26, 27, 29, 44, 57, 58, 59, 60
Chronology, 23, 26
Complex story, 71ff.
Component story, 72, 73, 74, 75, 76, 77, 78
Conjoining, 72, 76
Conjunctive feature, 18, 19, 20, 21, 22, 23, 24, 31, 32, 38, et passim
Conjunctive term, 18, 30, 32

Degree of grammaticalness, 10

Deighton, Len, 62
Dorfman, Eugene, 11
Dos Passos, John, 59
Ducasse, C. J., 42
Ducrot, Oswald, 11
Dundes, Alan, 10, 11, 12, 28

Embedding, 72, 73, 74, 76, 77
Episode, 45, 46, 47, 51, 65, 69
Erlich, Victor, 11
Event, 17, 18, 19, 20, 21, 22, 23, 24, 25, 26, et passim
Expression rules, 35, 36

Generalized transformation, 77, 78, 80, 81, 83, 101
Genette, Gérard, 63
Grammar G, 53, 56, 63, 64, 66, 69, 70, 80, 81
Grammar of kernel simple stories, 49-51
Grammar of minimal stories, 32, 34-35, 49
Grammar of stories, 5, 10, 11, 13, 15, 53, 69, 101
Greimas, A. J., 11, 20, 23
Guenoun, Denis, 12

Harris, Zellig, 51
Hendricks, William O., 11, 51

James, Henry, 49

Kernel simple story, 5, 38ff., 56, 63, 68, 69, 78

Köngas, Elli K., 11
Kristeva, Julia, 64

Labov, William, 46, 47
Lévi-Strauss, Claude, 11, 12
Logical order, 26, 27

Maranda, Pierre, 11
Mendilow, A. A., 23
Meredith, George, 49
Minimal story, 5, 16, 18ff., 38, 39, 40,
41, 44, 45, 47, et passim
Morin, Violette, 20

Narrative event, 40, 41, 42, 46, 61, 62,
63, 69, 71, 72, 73, 74
Narrative episode, 46, 65, 69
Narrativity, 41
Neumayer, Peter F., 9

Perrault, Charles, 5, 84
Peytard, Jean, 11
Pike, Kenneth L., 27
Postal, Paul, 10, 32
Pouillon, Jean, 23
Prince, Ellen F., 30
Prince, Gerald, 17, 25, 63
Propp, Vladimir, 10, 12, 16, 28, 63, 72
Proust, Marcel, 58, 77

Robbe-Grillet, Alain, 23, 24
Romains, Jules, 59

Sartre, Jean-Paul, 24, 43, 59
Scott, Charles T., 17
Sentence, 17, 18, 19, 20, 26, 29
Simple story, 56ff., 72, 73, 74, 75
Singulary transformation, 64, 68, 69,
70, 77, 78, 83, 100, 101
Spatial order, 26
Spatio-chronological order, 39, 40,
44, 45, 101
Spillane, Mickey, 43
Stative event, 29, 30, 31, 32, 41, 43, 47
Stative sentence, 30, 32
Story, 5, 9, 10, 11, 12, 13, 14, 15, 16,
17 et passim
Story order, 57, 58, 60
Storyness, 13

Todorov, Hristo, 47
Todorov, Tzvetan, 11, 12, 16, 17, 23,
27, 28, 31, 57, 58, 59, 72, 73, 74
Tomachevski, Boris, 16
Transform, 17, 18, 31
Transformational rules, 51, 53, 63, 64,
69, 70, 77, 80, 101

Van Dine, S. S., 43

Waletzky, Joshua, 46, 47
Woolf, Virginia, 49

Zeroed event, 60, 61, 62
Zeroing, 31, 62